A GIFT FOR:

_____

FROM:

_____

HOPE
FOR EVERY MOMENT

*365 Inspirational
Thoughts for Every Day
of the Year*

T.D. Jakes

Compiled by Jan Sherman

Destiny Image® Publishers, Inc.

P.O. Box 310

Shippensburg, PA 17257-0310

"Speaking to the Purposes of God for this Generation
and for the Generations to Come."

Hardcover Trade Edition:

ISBN 10: 0-7684-2397-X

ISBN 13: 978-0-7684-2397-6

Hardcover Special Edition:

ISBN 10: 0-7684-2424-0

ISBN 13: 978-0-7684-2424-9

For Worldwide Distribution

Printed in the U.S.A.

This book and all other Destiny Image, Revival Press, MercyPlace, Fresh Bread, Destiny Image Fiction, and Treasure House books are available at Christian bookstores and distributors worldwide.

3 4 5 6 7 8 9 10 / 10 09 08 07

For a U.S. bookstore nearest you, call
1-800-722-6774.

For more information on foreign distributors, call
717-532-3040.

Or reach us on the Internet:
www.destinyimage.com

*And, behold, there was a woman which had a spirit
of infirmity eighteen years, and was bowed together,
and could in no wise lift up herself...He called her
to Him, and said unto her, Woman, thou art loosed
from thine infirmity.*

Luke 13:11-12

Perhaps you will find some point of relativity between
her case history and your own. There are three major
characters in this story: the person, the problem and the
prescription. For every person, there will be a problem
and for every problem, our God has a prescription!

Jesus' opening statement to this woman is not a recom-
mendation for counseling—it is a challenging command!
Jesus did not counsel what should have been commanded. I am not against seeking the counsel of godly
men. The Scriptures say: *Where no counsel is, the people
fall: but in the multitude of counselor's there is safety*
(Proverbs 11:14).

After you have analyzed your condition and understood its origin, it will take the authority of God's
Word to put the past under your feet! Although the
problem may be rooted in the past, the prescription is a
present Word from God! The Word you hear today will
heal your yesterday!

*But if we walk in the light, as He is in the light…
the blood of Jesus Christ His Son cleanseth us from
all sin.*

1 John 1:7

The blood is the only element in the body that reaches, affects, and fuels all other parts of the body. If the blood is restricted long enough from any member of the body, that member will internally asphyxiate. Asphyxiated cells can quickly die—even without an external assailant—for their affliction is the result of internal deprivation.

Every limb and organ in the human body needs the blood. Along with its culinary duty of delivering soluble dietary contents throughout the body, our blood also functions as a paramedic. The white blood cells are uniquely equipped to fight off attacking bacteria and expel it from the body—stripping it of its power and robbing it of its spoils.

The physical body illustrates the power of the blood in the Church. Every member of the Body of Christ needs the life-giving blood of Jesus. Without the blood, we cease to have the proof of our sonship. Without His blood, we are pseudo-heirs trying to receive the promises reserved for the legitimate sons of God!

To every thing there is a season, and a time to every purpose under the heaven.

Ecclesiastes 3:1

We will always have seasons of struggles and testing. There are times when everything we attempt to do will seem to go wrong. Regardless of our prayers and consecration, adversity will come. We can't pray away God's seasons. The Lord has a purpose in not allowing us to be fruitful all the time.... When God sends the chilly winds of winter to blow on our circumstances, we must still trust Him.

The apostle Paul calls such times *"...light affliction, which is but for a moment..."* (2 Cor. 4:17). I say, "This too shall pass!" Some things you are not meant to change, but to survive. So if you can't alter it, then out-live it! Be like a tree. In the frosty arms of winter the forest silently refurbishes its strength, preparing for its next season of fruitfulness. In the spring it will push its way up into the budding of a new experience. Temporary setbacks create opportunities for fresh commitment and renewal. There are seasons of sunshine as well as rain. Each stage has its own purpose.

For God so loved the world, that He gave His only begotten Son.

John 3:16a

One of the first things that a hurting person needs to do is break the habit of using other people as a narcotic to numb the dull aching of an inner void. The more you medicate the symptoms, the less chance you have of allowing God to heal you. Avoid addictive, obsessive relationships.

If you are becoming increasingly dependent upon anything other than God to create a sense of wholeness in your life, then you are abusing your relationships. Clinging to people is far different from loving them. It is not so much a statement of your love for them as it is a crying out of your need for them. Like lust, it is intensely selfish. It is taking and not giving. Love is giving. God is love. God proved His love not by His need of us, but by His giving to us.

Sometimes we esteem others more important than ourselves. Watch out for self-disdain! If we don't apply some of the medicine that we use on others to strengthen ourselves, our patients will be healed and we will be dying.

...unto obedience and sprinkling of the blood of Jesus Christ: grace unto you, and peace, be multiplied.

1 Peter 1:2b

We did not need the blood only for when we cried out to the Lord to come into our hearts by faith. On the contrary, we still need that same blood today. All our strength and nourishment and every promise and miracle must flow to us through the blood. It gives us life from day to day!

We have lost our teaching of the blood in this age of Pentecostalism. We have learned about the Spirit of God, but we failed to teach about the blood. Consequently, we have produced a generation of believers who are empowered by the Spirit but do not feel forgiven! They are operating in the gifts, but living in guilt!

The blood must be preached. Without it we have no life. Why are we wasting the power of God on the problems of our past? The blood has already totally destroyed past bondages that held us down! It was through the eternal Spirit of God that Jesus was able to offer up His blood. There can be no Pentecost where there is no Passover!

Not by might, nor by power, but by My spirit, saith the Lord of hosts.

Zechariah 4:6b

For the vision is yet for an appointed time.

Habakkuk 2:3a

God is a God of order; He does everything by appointment. He has set a predetermined appointment to bring to pass His promise in our lives. Through the many tempestuous winds that blow against our lives, God has already prepared a way of escape. Our comfort is in knowing that we have an appointment with destiny. It is the inner awareness that makes us realize that in spite of temporary circumstances, God has a present time of deliverance.

We are enveloped in peace when we know that nothing the enemy does can abort the plan of God for our lives. The promise will come to pass. It will not be by human might or power, but by the Spirit of the Lord. David said, *"My times are in Thy hand"* (Ps. 31:15a). For me there is a sense of tranquility that comes from resting in the Lord. His appointment for us is predetermined. There is a peace that comes from knowing God has included us in His plan—even the details.

The Spirit of the Lord is upon Me, because He hath anointed Me.

Luke 4:18a

One of the many damaging things that can affect us today is divorce, particularly among women, who often look forward to a happy relationship. Whenever a woman is indoctrinated to think success is romance and then experiences the trauma of a failed relationship, she comes to a painful awakening. Divorce is not merely separating; it is the tearing apart of what was once joined together. Whenever something is torn, it does not heal easily. But Jesus can heal a broken or torn heart!

Approximately five out of ten marriages end in divorce. Broken homes leave a trail of broken dreams, people, and children. Only the Master can treat the long-term effects of this tragedy. One healing balm of the Holy Spirit is forgiveness. To forgive is to break the link between you and your past. Many times the person hardest to forgive is the one in the mirror. Regardless of who you hold responsible, there is no healing in blame! When you begin to realize that your past does not necessarily dictate the outcome of your future, then you can release the hurt.

*Now therefore ye are no more strangers and for-
eigners, but fellow citizens with the saints, and of
the household of God.*

Ephesians 2:19

There is a devilish prejudice in the Church that denies
the blood to its uncomely members. If a person has a
failure in an area we relate to because we have a similar
weakness, we immediately praise God for the blood that
cleanses us from all unrighteousness. If they are unfortunate enough to fail where we are very strong, then we
deny them the blood.

We have spilled our brother's blood because he is different, because his sin is different from ours. But by the
blood of the Lamb, any man, regardless of his failures or
past sin, can come equally and unashamedly to the foot
of the Cross and allow the drops of Jesus' blood to invig-
orate the soul that sin has lacerated and destroyed.

Have you ever been guilty of having a condescending attitude about another person's weakness? How can we dare to
think we can access the soul-cleansing blood that delivers
us from the cesspool of our secret sins, and then look down
on another member of Christ's Body in disdain?

I am God, and there is none like Me, declaring the end from the beginning, and from ancient times the things that are not yet done, saying, My counsel shall stand, and I will do all My pleasure.

Isaiah 46:9b-10

At the early age of six, I knew I had an appointment with destiny and that God had a purpose for my life. Somewhere in the recesses of your mind there should be an inner knowing that directs you toward an expected end. You must be the kind of tenacious person who can speak to the enemy and tell him, "My life can't end without certain things coming to pass. It's not over until God says, 'It's over!'"

I can't say that everything I encountered in life pushed me toward my destiny. On the contrary, there were sharp contradictions as I went through my tempestuous teens. Still, I had that inner knowing. I want you to know that even if circumstances contradict purpose, purpose will always prevail! It is the opposition that clearly demonstrates to you that God is working. When all indicators say it is impossible and it still occurs, then you know God has done it again.

I shall not die, but live, and declare the works of the Lord.

Psalm 118:17

One of the more serious indictments against our civilization is our flagrant disregard for the welfare of our children. Child abuse, regardless of whether it is physical, sexual, or emotional, is a terrible issue. It is horrifying to think that little children who survive the peril of the streets, the public schools, and the aggravated society in which we live, come home to be abused in what should be a haven. Recent statistics suggest that three in five young girls in this country have been or will be sexually assaulted.

Whenever I think on these issues, I am reminded of what my mother used to say. I was forever coming home with a scratch or cut from schoolyard play. My mother would take the Band-Aid off, clean the wound and say, "Things that are covered don't heal well."

It takes a lot of courage to receive ministry in sensitive areas. The Lord, though, is the kind of physician who can pour on the healing oil. Uncover your wounds in His presence and allow Him to gently heal the injuries.

Unto Adam also and to his wife did the Lord God make coats of skin, and clothed them.

Genesis 3:21

Because we have offered no provision for sons and daughters who fall, many of our Adams and our Eves are hiding in the bushes. Our fallen brethren hear our message, but they cannot come out to a preacher or a crowd that merely points out their nakedness and has nothing to cover them. We need to offer the perfect sacrifice to the sons of God as well as to the world. Adam was God's son. He was fallen and he was foolish, but he was the son of God!

The blood of Christ will even reach the falling, faltering son who hides in the bushes of our churches. Who will walk the cool of the garden to find him or to cover him? Many of us are taking the first walk to discover the fallen, but they have not taken the deeper walk to cover the fallen. When God covered Adam and Eve's nakedness, He covered what He discovered with the bloody skins of an innocent animal, giving Himself the first sacrifice to atone for their sin.

And Adam knew his wife again; and she bare a son, and called his name Seth: For God, said she, hath appointed me another seed instead of Abel, who Cain slew.

Genesis 4:25

When Eve produced what she thought to be the promised seed, there were real problems…. In the heat of rage, Cain killed his brother. She was supposed to be the mother of all living and all she had raised was a corpse and its murderer.

But God unwrapped the blanket of failure and blessed her with another son. She named him "Seth." Seth means "substituted."…Suddenly, as she held her new baby in her arms, she realized that God is sovereign. Eve called her third son "Seth," for she understood that if God makes a promise to bless someone, He will find a way! Even if it means appointing a substitute, He will perform His promise.

Ultimately everything God has ever said will come to pass. When we suffer loss like Eve did, we cannot allow past circumstances to abort future opportunity. If you have experienced loss in your life, God has a way of restoring things you thought you would never see again.

Do not conform any longer to the pattern of this world, but be transformed by the renewing of your mind. Then you will be able to test and approve what God's will is—His good, pleasing and perfect will.

Romans 12:2 NIV

Even when a victim survives, there is still a casualty. It is the death of trust. Little girls tend to be trusting and unsuspicious. When those who should nurture and protect them violate that trust through illicit behavior, multiple scars result. It is like programming a computer with false information; you can get out of it only what has been programmed into it.

It would be easy for this kind of scared little girl to grow into a young lady who has difficulty trusting anyone! Drug rehabilitation centers and prisons are full of adults who were abused children.

We frame our references around our own experiences. If those experiences are distorted, our ability to comprehend spiritual truths can be off center. What do you do when you have been poorly programmed by life's events? You can re-program your mind through the Word of God.

...by His own blood He [Christ] entered in once into the holy place, having obtained eternal redemption for us.

Hebrews 9:12b

Before Adam could receive the covering God had provided, though, he had to disrobe himself of what he had contrived. Adam stripped himself before a holy God, admitted his tragic sins, and still maintained his position as a son in the presence of God. Adam and Eve realized that the only solution for their sin was in the perfect provision of their loving God. That same loving God now reaches out to us as we are, and refashions us into what we should become!

We hear no further mention of blame or guilt concerning the first family as they walked away from the worst moment in the history of humanity. Why? They were wrapped and protected in the provision of God.

We, too, need to have this knowledge, regardless of whom we would want to blame or belittle. The disease is sin, the wage or prognosis is death, and the antidote prescribed is the blood and the blood alone. Never forget the blood, for without it we have no good news at all!

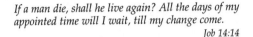

*If a man die, shall he live again? All the days of my
appointed time will I wait, till my change come.*

Job 14:14

It would be terrible to look back over your life and see
that the many times you thought your request was
denied was actually only delayed. Life will always present broken places, places of struggle and conflict. If you
have a divine purpose and life has put you on hold, hang
on! Stay on the line until life gets back to you. It's worth
the wait to receive your answer from the Lord.

The real test of faith is in facing the silence of being on
hold. Those are the suspended times of indecision. Have
you felt you were on the verge of something phenome-
nal, that you were waiting for that particular breakthrough that seemed to be taunting you by making you
wait? All of us have faced days that seemed as though
God had forgotten us. These are the moments that feel
like eternity. Patience gets a workout when God's answer
is no answer. In other words, God's answer is not always
yes or no; sometimes He says, "Not now!"

Sanctify them through Thy truth: Thy word is truth.
John 17:17

———

Y̲ou can have a complete metamorphosis through the Word of God. It has been my experience, who does extensive counseling in my own ministry and abroad, that many abused people, women in particular, tend to flock to legalistic churches who see God primarily as a disciplinarian. Many times the concept of fatherhood for them is a harsh code of ethics. This type of domineering ministry may appeal to those who are performance-oriented. I understand that morality is important in Christianity; however, there is a great deal of difference between morality and legalism. It is important that God not be misrepresented. He is a balanced God, not an extremist.

The glory of God is manifested only when there is a balance between grace and truth. Religion doesn't transform. Legalism doesn't transform. For the person who feels dirty, harsh rules could create a sense of self-righteousness. God doesn't have to punish you to heal you.

Believe the Word of God and be free. Jesus was a great emancipator of the oppressed. It does not matter whether someone has been oppressed socially, sexually, or racially; our Lord is an eliminator of distinctions.

But God commendeth His love toward us, in that, while we were yet sinners, Christ died for us.

Romans 5:8

I can't help but wonder what would happen if we would ever love like Jesus loves…. As we peel away layer by layer, as we become more comfortable with our God and our own humanity, we become increasingly transparent. We must achieve a level of honesty that will keep us from being estranged from our important relationships. We have to love and be loved by someone to the degree that we can say, "This is who I am, and it is all that I am. Love me and be patient with me. There is no telling what I will become, but today this is who I am."

When you find someone who can see your flaws and your underdeveloped character, and love you in spite of it all, you are blessed. If the only way you can love me is after I have perfected my imperfections, then you really don't love me. God loved you while you were unlovable so you would never have to hide in the bushes again! He has loved you with an everlasting love!

Wait on the Lord; be of good courage, and He shall strengthen thine heart: wait, I say, on the Lord.

Psalm 27:14

It is God's timing that we must learn. He synchronizes His answers to accomplish His purpose. While traveling on a major American airline, we were told that the plane could not land and we had to wait in the air. I have often felt like that aircraft suspended in the air when God says, "Wait!"

There was a calm assurance on the faces of the flight attendants. I would have to attribute it to the fact that they had prepared for a delay. I began to wonder if we shouldn't be better prepared for those times when God puts us in a holding pattern. Do you have enough faith to assume a holding pattern and wait for the fulfillment of the promise?

You feel a deep sense of contentment when you know God has not forgotten you. I will never forget the time I went through a tremendous struggle. I thought it was an emergency. I thought I had to have an answer right then. I learned that God isn't easily spooked by what I call an emergency.

Or despisest thou the riches of his goodness and for-bearance and longsuffering; not knowing that the goodness of God leadeth thee to repentance?

Romans 2:4

Repentance doesn't come because of the scare tactics and threats of raging ministers who need mercy themselves. Repentance comes because of the unfailing love of a perfect God, a God who cares for the cracked vases that others would have discarded. It is His great love that causes a decision to be made in the heart: I must live for Him!

There is no way that you can see Him stand with you when all others forsake you, and not want to please Him! There is no way you can weather a storm in His loving arms and not say, "I am Yours, O Lord. Such as I have I give to You." One gaze into His holiness will bring the sinner crashing to the floor on bended knees, confessing and forsaking every issue that could have engulfed him.

In other words, God is too good for us to experience His love and then be contented to abuse that love. If nowhere else, and by no one else, you are accepted in the beloved!

> *There is neither Jew or Greek* [racial], *there is neither bond nor free* [social]. *There is neither male nor female* [sexual]: *for ye are all one in Christ Jesus.*
>
> *Galatians 3:28*

Unity should not come at the expense of uniqueness of expression. We should also tolerate variance in social classes. The Church is not an elite organization for spiritual yuppies only, one that excludes other social classes.

If uniqueness is to be appreciated racially and socially, it is certainly to be appreciated sexually. Male and female are one in Christ. Yet they are unique and that uniqueness is not to be tampered with. It is a sin for a man to misrepresent himself by conducting himself as a woman. I am not merely speaking of homosexuality. I am also talking about men who are feminine in their mannerisms. It is equally sad to see a masculine woman. Nevertheless, God wants them healed, not hated!

God can appreciate our differences and still create unity. It is like a conductor who can orchestrate extremely different instruments into producing a harmonious, unified sound. Together we produce a sound of harmony that expresses the multifaceted character of God.

Work out your own salvation with fear and trembling. For it is God which worketh in you both to will and to do of His good pleasure.

Philippians 2:12b-13

God is too good for us to experience His love and then be contented to abuse that love. Accepting the rejected is not the weakness of the Gospel; it is its strength! It is to the distraught heart that seeks so desperately for a place of refuge that we extend soft hands and tender words.

How can we then define the Church, with its rising divorce rate and afflicted leadership? The Church needs to bathe itself in its own message. We have strengths and struggles. We have boxed ourselves in and lifted ourselves up as the epitome of sanctity. But beneath our stained glass windows and padded pews lie broken hearts and torn families.

We have no right to be blessed, in ourselves. Yet He has blessed us "in spite of us." Beneath the streaming tears of a grateful heart, through our trembling lips must emerge the birthing thoughts that Christ has done it all, and that we have nothing to boast in but His precious blood alone!

*For He knoweth our future; He remembereth that
we are dust.*

Psalm 103:14

O nce while struggling to understand why God had not
more readily answered one of my requests, I stumbled upon a word that brought streams into my desert.

*But God remembered Noah...and He sent a wind
over the earth, and the waters receded.*

Genesis 8:1 NIV

The first four words were all I needed. When you realize
that God knows where you are and that He will get back
to you in time—what peace, what joy! Before Noah ran
out of resources and provisions, God remembered him!
The Lord knows where you are and He knows how much
you have left in reserve. Just before you run out, God
will send the wind to blow back the waters of impossibil-
ity and provide for you.

I, too, need ministry to keep my attitude from falling
while I wait on the manifestation of the promise of God.
Sometimes very simplistic reminders that God is still
sovereign bring great joy to the heart of someone who is
in a holding pattern. The comforting Spirit of God
calms my fears every time He reminds me that God
doesn't forget.

And being found in fashion as a man, He humbled Himself, and became obedient unto death, even the death of the cross.

Philippians 2:8

To fully understand the precious effect of Jesus' blood, we must take a look back at Calvary's bloody banks. Look at the 33-year-old body that was filled with such youth and potential now hangs from a cross like a slab of unused meat. From His beaten back to His ripped torso, we see a wounded knight without armor. His garments lie crumbled on the ground, the object of the desires of His villainous guards who now gamble up their leisure moments, waiting on the death angel to flap his wings in the face of the Savior.

When you look at this icon of grace, remove your religious glasses and you will see a sweat-drenched, trembling, bleeding offering. He hung dying as if He were the bastard son of Mary, not the King that He was—dying like a thief in the night! That crucifixion was a debauchery and degradation so horrible that it embarrassed the sun into hiding its face and made the ground tremble at the nervous sight of the King of glory.

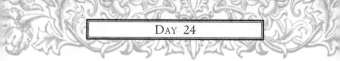

Submit yourselves, then, to God. Resist the devil,
and he will flee from you.

James 4:7 NIV

By nature a woman is a receiver. She is not physically
designed to be a giver. Her sexual and emotional fulfillment becomes somewhat dependent on the giving of
her male counterpart (in regard to intimate relationships). There is a certain vulnerability that is part of
being a receiver. In regard to reproduction (sexual relationships), the man is the contributing factor, and the
woman is the receiver.

What is true of the natural is true of the spiritual. Men
tend to act out of what they perceive to be facts, while
women tend to react out of their emotions. If your
actions and moods are not a reaction to the probing of
the Holy Spirit, then you are reacting to the subtle taunting of the enemy. He is trying to produce his destructive
fruit in your home, heart, and even in your relationships.
Receiver, be careful what you receive! Moods and attitudes that satan offers, you need to resist. It is his job to
offer it and your job to resist it. If you do your job, all
will go well.

And killed the Prince of life, whom God hath raised from the dead; whereof we are witnesses.

Acts 3:15

To me, Jesus Christ is the Prince of Peace. But to them, He was the entertainment for the evening. They stripped Him completely and totally. They humiliated Him by placing a robe upon His nude body and a crown upon His head. Then they amused themselves with Him. They led Him away to the Cross. At the Cross, Jesus again was stripped of His own clothes like the innocent animal in the Book of Genesis was stripped of its coat of skin.

Likewise, Jesus was made bare that I might be covered. Climbing naked upon the Cross, He was nailed to a tree! They then parted His garments among themselves and watched Him, naked and not ashamed! They watched until grace grew weary and mercifully draped a curtain over the sun, allowing darkness to veil Him from the watchful eyes of unconcerned hearts. These are the eyes of coldhearted men, men whose eyes are still darkened today lest they behold the wonder of His glory. That is why they can't quite see what we see when we look at Calvary!

> *For I know the thoughts that I think toward you,*
> *saith the Lord, thoughts of peace, and not of evil, to*
> *give you an expected end.*
>
> *Jeremiah 29:11*

When Noah had been held up long enough to accomplish what was necessary for his good, God sent the wind. There is a wind that comes from the Presence of God. It blows back the hindrances and dries the ground beneath your feet. Whenever the breath of the Almighty breathes a fresh anointing on you, it is an indication of a supernatural deliverance.

Regardless of the obstacle in your life, the wind from God can bring you out. Let the His wind blow down every spirit of fear and heaviness that would cause you to give up on what God has promised you. The description of the Holy Spirit says He is as *"a rushing mighty wind"* (Acts 2:2). For every mighty problem in your life, there is a mighty rushing wind! Now, a normal wind can be blocked out but the gusty wind from the Lord is too strong to be controlled. It will blow back the Red Sea. God's wind is ultra-effective against every current event in your life.

Neither give place to the devil.

Ephesians 4:27

It is not enough to reject the enemy's plan. You must nurture the Word of the Lord. You need to draw the promise of God and the vision for the future to your breast. It is a natural law that anything not fed will die. Caution: Be sure you are nurturing what you want to grow and starving what you want to die.

As you read this, you may feel that life is passing you by. You often experience success in one area and gross defeat in others. You need a burning desire for the future, the kind of desire that overcomes past fear and inhibitions. You will remain chained to your past and all the secrets therein until you decide: Enough is enough!

I am telling you that when your desire for the future peaks, you can break out of prison. I challenge you to sit down and write 30 things you would like to do with your life and scratch them off, one by one, as you accomplish them. There is no way you can plan for the future and dwell in the past at the same time.

Who His own self bare our sins in His own body on the tree, that we, being dead to sins, should live unto righteousness: by whose stripes ye were healed.

1 Peter 2:24

The Savior's head is pricked with the thorns of every issue that would ever rest on my mind. His hands are nailed through for every vile thing I have ever used mine to do. His feet are nailed to the tree for every illicit, immoral place you and I have ever walked! In spite of His pain and abuse, in spite of His torment and His nudity, He was still preaching as they watched Him dying—naked and not ashamed!

Why is a loincloth painted on most of the pictures I see of Jesus on the Cross? Isn't that what hinders us now? Are we, the Body of Christ, hiding beneath a loincloth that has stifled our testimony and blocked our ability to be transparent, even with one another? We have not been allowed to share our struggles as well as our successes. Beneath the loincloth of human expectation and excessive demands, many men and women are bleeding to death!

For we have not an high priest which cannot be touched with the feeling of our infirmities; but was ion all points tempted like as we are, yet without sin.

Hebrews 4:15

Have you ever noticed how hard it is to communicate with people who will not give you their attention? Pain will not continue to rehearse itself in the life of a preoccupied, distracted person. Distracted people do not respond! Every woman has something she wishes she could forget. Forgetting isn't a memory lapse; it is a memory release! Like carbon dioxide the body can no longer use, exhale it and let it go out of your spirit.

God cares, sees and calls the infirm to the dispensary of healing and deliverance. Like a 24-hour medical center, you can reach Him at anytime. He is touched by the feeling of your infirmity....

I pray that the Holy Spirit would roll you into the recovery room where you can fully realize that the trauma is over. I am excited to say that God never loosed anybody that He wasn't going to use mightily. May God reveal healing and purpose as we continue to seek Him.

The Lord hath made bare His holy arm in the eyes of
all the nations; and all the ends of the earth shall see
the salvation of our God.

Isaiah 52:10

Again, I see the tragedy in the fact that the loincloth represents all those things that are humanly imposed upon us, things that God does not require!

I resent the loincloth because it is almost prophetic of what the Church, the mystical Body of Christ, has done today. We have hidden our humanity beneath the man-made cloths of religiosity. We have covered up what God has made bare! We need no loincloth; the Body of Christ was meant to be naked and not ashamed. His provision for our nudity was His blood.

I hope you have only one defense when it is your turn to go on trial. Do not submit a loincloth for evidence; it is inadmissible. But my wounded, hurting, healing, helping, giving, and needing friend, when they try your case (and they surely will), open your mouth, clear your throat, and plead, "No additives; the blood alone"!

But the scripture hath concluded all under sin, that the promise by faith of Jesus Christ might be given to them that believe.

Galatians 3:22

Many Christians experienced the new birth early in their childhood. It is beneficial to have the advantage of Christian ethics. I'm not sure what it would have been like to have been raised in the church and been insulated from worldliness and sin. Sometimes I envy those who have been able to live victoriously all of their lives. Most of us have not had that kind of life. My concern is the many persons who have lost their sensitivity for others and who suffer from spiritual arrogance. Jesus condemned the Pharisees for their spiritual arrogance, yet many times that self-righteous spirit creeps into the Church.

The fact is, we were all born in sin and shaped in iniquity. We have no true badge of righteousness that we can wear on the outside. God concluded all are in sin so He might save us from ourselves. We were born in sin, equally and individually shaped in iniquity, and not one race or sociological group has escaped the fact that we are Adam's sinful heritage.

For a just man falleth seven times, and riseth up again: but the wicked shall fall into mischief.

Proverbs 24:16

Sometimes Christians become frustrated and with-draw from activity on the basis of personal strug-gles. They think it's all over, but God says not so! The best is yet to come. But if you want the Lord to come, you mustn't tell Him that you aren't planning to get up.

The whole theme of Christianity is one of rising again. However, you can't rise until you fall. Now that doesn't mean you should fall into sin. It means you should allow the resurrecting power of the Holy Ghost to operate in your life regardless of whether you have fallen into sin, discouragement, apathy, or fear. But it doesn't matter what tripped you; it matters that you rise up. People who never experience these things generally are people who don't do anything. There is a certain safety in being dor-mant. Nothing is won, but nothing is lost. I would rather walk on the water with Jesus. I would rather nearly drown and have to be saved than play it safe and never experience the miraculous.

To the praise of the glory of His grace, wherein He hath made us accepted in the beloved.

Ephesians 1:6

I remember, in my early days as a new Christian, that I tried to become what I thought all the other Christians were. I didn't understand that my goal should have been to achieve God's purpose for my life. I was young and so impressionable. Suffering from low self-esteem, I thought that the Christians around me had mastered a level of holiness that seemed to evade me. They seemed so changed, so sure, and so stable! I earnestly prayed, "Make me better, Lord"!

I don't think I have changed that prayer, but I have changed the motivation behind it. I had always been surrounded by a love that was based upon performance. So I thought God's love was doled out according to a merit system. If I did well today, God loved me. However, if I failed, He did not love me. I didn't know whether I was accepted in the beloved, or not! Suddenly, I began to realize that God loved me as I was, although I had never been taught about perfect love.

For all have sinned and come short of the glory of God.

Romans 3:23

No one person needs any more of the blood of Jesus than the other. Jesus died once and for all. Humanity must come to God on equal terms, each individual totally helpless to earn his or her way to Him. When we come to Him with this attitude, He raises us up by the blood of Christ. He doesn't raise us up because we do good things. He raises us up because we have faith in the finished work on the Cross.

Many in the Church were striving for holiness. We were trying to perfect flesh. Flesh is in enmity against God, whether we paint it or not.

What is holiness? To understand it, we must first separate the pseudo from the genuine because, when you come into a church, it is possible to walk away feeling like a second-class citizen. Many start going overboard trying to be a super spiritual person in order to compensate for an embarrassing past. You can't earn deliverance. You have to just receive it by faith. Christ is the only righteousness that God will accept.

And He said unto me, My grace is sufficient for thee: for My strength is made perfect in weakness.
2 Corinthians 12:9a

When the AIDS epidemic hit this country, pandemonium erupted. Terror caused many people, Christians as well as non-Christians, to react out of ignorance and intimidation. People were whispering, wanting to know how it was contracted. In my church it is absolutely absurd to concern themselves with how anybody contracted AIDS. The issue is, they have it and what are we going to do to help.

If we intend to accomplish anything, we must react to adversity like yeast. Once yeast is thoroughly stirred into the dough, it cannot be detected. Although it is invisible, it is highly effective. When the heat is on, it will rise. The warmer the circumstance, the greater the reaction. Likewise, God sets us in warm, uncomfortable places so we can rise. Sometimes the worst times in our lives do more to strengthen us than all our mountaintop experiences. The power of God reacts to struggle and stress. Isn't that what God meant when He told Paul, *"...My strength is made perfect in weakness."*

All scripture is given by inspiration of God, and is profitable for doctrine, for reproof, for correction, for instruction in righteousness: that the man of God may be perfect, thoroughly furnished unto all good works.

2 Timothy 3:16,17

When I was saved, no one shared with me that they had experienced struggles before they obtained victories. No one told me that wars come before success.

I tried to measure up to others and answer all the concerns that plagued my heart. I felt ashamed. My heart cried out, "What must I do to be perfected in the Lord"?

It is important for us to let God mature us—without our self-help efforts to impress others with a false sense of piety. That kind of do-it-yourself righteousness and religion keeps us from being naked before God and from being comfortable with our own level of growth. Yes, I want to be all that God wants me to be. But while I am developing at the rate He has chosen, I will certainly thank Him for His rich grace and bountiful mercy along the way. This is the divine mercy that lets us mature naturally.

And He said unto me, My grace is sufficient for thee: for My strength is made perfect in weakness.
2 Corinthians 12:9

There is a sanctity of your spirit that comes through the blood of the Lord Jesus Christ and sanctifies the innermost part of your being. Certainly, once you get cleaned up in your spirit, it will be reflected in your character and conduct. The Spirit of the Lord will give you boundaries. People must be loosed from the chains of guilt and condemnation. Many women in particular have been bound by manipulative messages that specialize in control and dominance.

The Church must open its doors and allow people who have a past to enter in. The Bible never camouflaged the weaknesses of the people God used. God used David. God used Abraham. We must divorce our embarrassment about wounded people. Yes, we've got wounded people. Yes, we've got hurting people. Sometimes they break the boundaries and they become lascivious and out of control and we have to readmit them into the hospital and allow them to be treated again. That's what the Church is designed to do. The Church is a hospital for wounded souls.

Not only so, but we also rejoice in our sufferings, because we know that suffering produces persever-ance; perseverance, character; and character, hope.

Romans 5:3-4 NIV

Relentless is a word I use to describe people who will not take no for an answer! They try things one way, and if that doesn't work, they try it another way. But they don't give up. You who are about to break beneath the stress of intense struggles—be relentless! Do not quit!

A terrible thing happens to people who give up too eas-ily. It is called regret. It is the nagging, gnawing feeling that says, "If I had tried harder, I could have succeeded." Granted, we all experience some degree of failure. That is how we learn and grow. The problem isn't failure; it is when we fail and question if it was our lack of commit-ment that allowed us to forfeit an opportunity to turn the test into a triumph! We can never be sure of the answer unless we rally our talents, muster our courage, and focus our strength to achieve a goal. If we don't have the passion to be relentless, then we should leave it alone.

But we have this treasure in earthen vessels, that the excellency of the power may be of God, and not of us.

2 Corinthians 4:7

Many Christians struggle to produce a premature change when God-ordained change can only be accomplished according to His time. We cannot expect to change the flesh. It will not respond to therapy. God intends for us to grow spiritually while we live in our vile, corrupt flesh. While we are changed in our spirit by the new birth, our old corruptible body and fleshly desires are not. It is His will that our treasure be displayed in a cabinet of putrid, unregenerated flesh—openly displaying the strange dichotomy between the temporal and the eternal.

It is amazing that God would put so much in so little. The true wonder of His glory is painted on the dark canvas of our old personhood. What a glorious backdrop our weakness makes for His strength!

There is a great deal of power released through the friction of the holy graces of God grating against the dry, gritty surface of human incapacities and limitations. We sharpen our testimonies whenever we press His glory against our struggles.

[Jesus said] *"Come unto Me, all ye that labor and are heavy laden, and I will give you rest."*

Matthew 11:28

We have all wrestled with something, though it may not always be the same challenge. My struggle may not be yours. If I'm wrestling with something that's not a problem to you, you do not have the responsibility for judging me when all the while you are wrestling with something equally as incriminating.

Regardless of what a person has done, or what kind of abuse one has suffered, God still calls. Rest assured that He knows all about our secrets, and still draws us with an immutable call.

No matter how difficult life seems, people with a past need to make their way to Jesus. Regardless of the obstacles within and without, they must reach Him. You may have a baby out of wedlock cradled in your arms, but keep pressing on. You may have been abused and molested and never able to talk to anyone about it, but don't cease reaching out for Him. You don't have to tell everyone your entire history. He knows your history, but He called you anyway.

Even so ye, foreasmuch as ye are zealous of spiritual gifts, seek that ye may excel to the edifying of the church.

1 Corinthians 14:12

You would be surprised to know how many people there are who never focus on a goal. They do several things haphazardly without examining how forceful they can be when they totally commit themselves to a cause. The difference between the masterful and the mediocre is often a focused effort. On the other hand, mediocrity is masterful to persons of limited resources and abilities. So in reality, true success is relative to ability. What is a miraculous occurrence for one person can be nothing of consequence to another. A person's goal must be set on the basis of his ability to cultivate talents and his agility in provoking a change.

I am convinced that I have not fully developed my giftings. I am committed to being all that I was intended and predestined to be for the Lord, for my family, and for myself. How about you—have you decided to roll up your sleeves and go to work? Remember, effort is the bridge between mediocrity and masterful accomplishment!

In whom all the building fitly framed together growth unto an holy temple in the Lord: in whom also are builded together for an habitation of God through the Spirit.

Ephesians 2:21-22

———

Within our decaying shells, we constantly peel away, by faith, the lusts and jealousies that adorn the walls of our hearts. If the angels were to stroll through the earth with the Creator and ask, "Which house is Yours?" He would pass by all the mansions and cathedrals, all the temples and castles. Unashamedly, He would point at you and me and say, "That house is Mine!"

Yes, it is true: Despite all our washing and painting, this old house is still falling apart! We train it and teach it. We desperately try to convince it to at least think differently. But like a squeaky hinge on a swollen door, the results of our efforts, at best, come slowly. The Holy Ghost Himself resides beneath this sagging roof.

God Himself has—of His own free will and predetermined purpose—put us in the embarrassing situation of entertaining a Guest whose lofty stature so far exceeds us that we hardly know how to serve Him!

> *As for me, I will call upon God; and the Lord shall save me. Evening, and morning, and at noon, will I pray, and cry aloud: and He shall hear my voice. He hath delivered my soul in peace....*
>
> *Psalm 55:16-18a*

Jesus' actions were massively different from ours. He focused on helping hurting people. Every time He saw a hurting person, He reached out and ministered to their need. Once when He was preaching, He looked through the crowd and saw a man with a withered hand. He immediately healed him (see Mark 3:1-5). He sat with the prostitutes and the winebibbers, not the upper echelon of His community. Jesus surrounded Himself with broken, bleeding, dirty people. He called a woman who was crippled and bent over (see Luke 13:11-13). She had come to church and sat in the synagogue for years and years and nobody had helped that woman until Jesus saw her. He called her to the forefront.

Why didn't He speak the word and heal her in her seat? Perhaps God wants to see us moving toward Him. We need to invest in our own deliverance. We will bring a testimony out of a test.

But I keep under my body, and bring it into subjection: lest that by any means, when I have preached to others, I myself should be a castaway.

1 Corinthians 9:27

Our struggle is to continuously feed the ravenous appetite of the Holy Ghost. He daily consumes, and continually requires, that which we alone know God wants from us. Paul battled to bring into submission the hidden things in his life that could bring destruction. Perhaps they were putrid thoughts, or vain imaginations, or pride; but whatever they were, he declared war on them if they resisted change. He says, in essence, that as he waits for the change, he keeps his body in chains, beating back the forces of evil.

This is the struggle of the same man who wrote the majority of the New Testament! With a testimony like this, I pay very little attention to those among us who feel obligated to impress us with the ludicrous idea that they have already attained what is meant to be a lifelong pursuit. The renewal of the old man is a daily exercise of the heart. It progressively strengthens the character day by day, not overnight!

For He has rescued us from the dominion of darkness and brought us into the kingdom of the Son He loves.

Colossians 1:13 NIV

Many of the people who were a part of the ministry of Jesus' earthly life were people with colorful pasts. Some had indeed always looked for the Messiah to come. Others were involved in things that were immoral and inappropriate.

A good example is Matthew. He was a man who worked in an extremely distasteful profession. He was a tax collector. Few people like tax collectors still today. Their reputation was even worse at that time in history. Matthew collected taxes for the Roman empire. He had to have been considered a traitor by those who were faithful Jews. Romans were their oppressors. How could he have forsaken his heritage and joined the Romans? Regardless of his past, Jesus called Matthew to be a disciple. We must maintain a strong line of demarcation between a person's past and present.

These were the people Jesus wanted to reach. He was criticized for being around questionable characters. Everywhere He went the oppressed and the rejected followed Him. They knew that He offered mercy and forgiveness.

Who hath saved us, and called us with an holy call-
ing, not according to our works, but according to
His own purpose and grace, which was given us in
Christ Jesus before the world began.

2 Timothy 1:9

If you are only talented, you may feel comfortable taking your talents into a secular arena. Talent, like justice, is blind; it will seek all opportunities the same. But
when you are cognizant of divine purpose, there are
some things you will not do because they would defeat
the purpose of God in your life! Being called according
to purpose enables you to focus on the development of
your talent as it relates to your purpose!

Whenever we bring our efforts into alignment with His
purpose, we automatically are blessed. Our efforts must
be tailored after the pattern of divine purpose. Everyone
is already blessed. We often spend hours in prayer trying
to convince God that He should bless what we are trying
to accomplish. What we need to do is spend hours in
prayer for God to reveal His purpose. When we do what
God has ordained to be done, we are blessed because
God's plan is already blessed.

Now we know that if the earthly tent we live in is destroyed, we have a building from God, an eternal house in heaven, not built by human hands…. Now it is God who has…given us the Spirit as a deposit, guaranteeing what is to come.

2 Corinthians 5:1-15

So the bad news is that the old house is still a death trap; it's still infested with rodents. A legion of thoughts and pesky memories crawl around in our heads like roaches that come out in the night and boldly parade around the house. That should not negate our joy, though; it merely confesses our struggles.

The Guest we entertain desires more for us than what we have in us! He enjoys neither the house nor the clothing we offer Him. Jesus said, *"…every city or house divided against itself shall not stand"* (Matt. 12:25). Ever since we were saved, there has been a division in the house. Eventually the old house will have to yield to the new one! Yes, we are constantly renovating through the Word of God, but the truth is that God will eventually recycle what you and I have been trying to renovate!

For I delight in the law of God after the inward man: but I see another law in my members, warring against the law of my mind, and bringing me into captivity to the law of sin which is in my members.

Romans 7:22-23

Christianity means conflict. At the least, if it doesn't mean conflict, it certainly creates conflict! Living holy isn't natural. It isn't natural—it is spiritual! Unless we walk consistently in the spirit, living holy is difficult. No, it is impossible!

Without God it cannot be done! Being a Christian means that one part of you is constantly wanting to do the right thing while the other part of you is desperately campaigning for you to walk in your old habits. After I was saved, I didn't commit those wicked sins, but I would have had He not set up a protest in my heart! He brought my trembling soul to His bleeding side and cleansed my very imaginations, intentions, and ambitions! Yes, the Christian life is a life of conflict, and I thank God that He groans and protests my sinful behavior. It is because He challenges my proclivities that growth begins!

Stand fast therefore in the liberty wherewith Christ hath made us free, and be not entangled again with the yoke of bondage.

Galatians 5:1

When Christ taught in the temple courts, there were those who tried to trap Him in His words. They knew that His ministry appealed to the masses of lowly people. They thought that if they could get Him to say some condemning things, the people wouldn't follow Him anymore....

The blood of Jesus is efficacious, cleansing the woman who feels unclean. How can we reject what He has cleansed and made whole? Just as He said to the woman then, He proclaims today, *"Neither do I condemn thee: go and sin no more."* How can the Church do any less?

The chains that bind are often from events that we have no control over. Other times the chains are there because we have willfully lived lives that bring bondage and pain.

Regardless of the source, Jesus comes to set us free. He is unleashing the women of His Church. He forgives, heals, and restores. Women can find the potential of their future because of His wonderful power operating in their lives.

O Lord, how many are me foes! ...But You are a
shield around me, O Lord; You bestow glory on me
and lift up my head. To the Lord I cry aloud, and
He answers me from His holy hill. Selah.

Psalm 3:1-4 NIV

David declares that it is the Lord who sustains you in the perilous times of inner struggle and warfare. It is the precious peace of God that eases your tension when you are trying to make decisions in the face of criticism and cynicism. When you realize that some people do not want you to be successful, the pressure mounts drastically. Many have said, "God will not deliver him." However, many saying it still doesn't make it true. I believe that the safest place in the whole world is in the will of God. If you align your plan with His purpose, success is imminent! On the other hand, if I have not been as successful as I would like to be, then seeking the purpose of God inevitably enriches my resources and makes the impossible attainable.

If the storm comes and I know I am in the will of God, then little else matters.

*Against Thee, Thee only, have I sinned, and done
this evil in Thy sight: that Thou mightest be justified when Thou speakest, and be clear when Thou
judgest.*

Psalm 51:4

Saul was anointed by God to be king. He was more moral than David in that he didn't struggle in some of the areas that plagued David. His weakness wasn't outward; it was inward. Saul looked like a king, whereas David looked like an underage juvenile delinquent who should have been home taking care of the flocks. Saul's armor shined in the noonday sun. David had no armor. Even his weapon looked substandard; it was just an old, ragged, shepherd's slingshot.

Although David's weapon was outwardly substandard, it was nevertheless lethal; it led to the destruction of the giant. We can never destroy our enemy with the superficial armor of a pious king. We don't need the superficial. We need the supernatural! David's naked, transparent demeanor was so translucent that he often seems extremely vulnerable. You would almost think he was unfit, except that when he repents, there is something so powerful in his prayer that even his most adamant critic must admire his openness with God!

And the scribes and Pharisees brought unto Him a woman taken in adultery; and when they had set her in the midst, they say unto Him, Master, this woman was taken in adultery, in the very act…. So when they continued asking Him, He lifted up Himself, and said unto them, He that is without sin among you, let him first cast a stone at her.

John 8:3-7

Clearly Jesus saw the foolish religious pride in their hearts. He was not condoning the sin of adultery. He simply understood the need to meet people where they were and minister to their need. He saw the pride in the Pharisees and ministered correction to that pride. He saw the wounded woman and ministered forgiveness. Justice demanded that she be stoned to death. Mercy threw the case out of court. Jesus, however, knew the power of a second chance.

There are those today who are very much like this woman. They have come into the Church. They have been stoned and ridiculed. They may not be physically broken and bowed over, but they are wounded within. Somehow the Church must find room to throw off condemnation and give life and healing.

And Saul said unto Samuel, I have sinned: for I have transgressed the commandment of the Lord, and thy words: because I feared the people, and obeyed their voice.

1 Samuel 15:24

What a sharp contrast there is between David and King Saul, whose stately demeanor and pompous gait didn't stop him from being an incredible deceiver. Even when face-to-face with Samuel the prophet, Saul lied at a time he should have repented! The problem with people like Saul is that they are more interested in their image than they are concerned about being immaculate in their hearts.

While Saul stood arrayed in his kingly attire, boasting of his conquest over an enemy king and lying about his real struggles, the heathen king whom Saul had been commanded to kill was still alive. The sheep that he had been ordered to destroy were still bleating in the valley. God did not destroy Saul for not killing what he should have killed; that wasn't the biggest problem. The central problem was that Saul's deceitfulness had become a breach too wide to bridge. David might have been weak and struggled with moral issues, but at least he was naked before God!

As one whom his mother comforteth, so will I comfort you; and ye shall be comforted in Jerusalem.

Isaiah 66:13

I remember when our car broke down. It didn't have too far to break down because it already was at death's door. At the time, though, I needed to get uptown to ask the electric company not to cut off the only utility I had left. I pleaded with them but they cut it off anyway. I was crushed. I had been laid off my job, and my church was so poor it couldn't even pay attention. I walked out of the utility office and burst into tears. I looked like an insane person walking down the street. I was at the end of my rope.

To this melodramatic outburst God said absolutely nothing. He waited until I had gained some slight level of composure and then spoke. He said, "I will not suffer thy foot to be moved!" I shall never forget as long as I live the peace of His promise that came into my spirit. Suddenly the light, the gas, and the money didn't matter. What mattered was I knew I was not alone.

*He that worketh deceit shall not dwell within my
house: he that telleth lies shall not tarry in my sight.*

Psalm 101:7

Saul had a terrible character flaw, that of deceit....
Even when he was face-to-face with Samuel the
prophet, Saul lied when he should have repented! (See
First Samuel 15:15-24.) ...Saul represents that part of
all of us that must be overthrown. We must renounce
deceit if we are to go beyond the superficial and fulfill
our destiny in the supernatural. There must be an open
confession that enables God's grace to be allocated to
your need.

There is a gradual transference of authority as we walk
with God. We move from the Saul-like rule of superficial
religion to a Davidic anointing based on honesty and
transparency.

Only God knows the process it will take for Christ to
be formed in you. He is taking each of us to that place
where the child begins to bear a greater resemblance to
his Father. Be assured that this only occurs at the end
of travailing prayer and openness of heart, as we confess and forsake every trace of Saul's rule in our lives.

*Thou has known my reproach, and my shame, and
my dishonour: mine adversaries are all before Thee.*

Psalm 69:19

Israel was at its zenith under the leadership of a godly
king named David. There can be no argument that
David frequently allowed his passions to lead him into
moral failure. However, he was a man who recognized
his failures and repented. He was a man who sought
God's heart.

Although David longed to follow God, some of his passions and lust were inherited by his children. Maybe they
learned negative things from their father's failures. That
is a tendency we must resist. We ought not repeat the
failure of our fathers. We are most vulnerable, however,
to our father's weaknesses. David's son, Amnon, demon-
strated one of these weaknesses as he shamed his half-
sister, Tamar, by raping her.

The name Tamar means "palm tree." Tamar is a survivor.
She still stands. When the cold blight of winter stands up
in her face, she withstands the chilly winds and remains
green throughout the winter. Tamar is a survivor. You are
a survivor. Through hard times God has granted you the
tenacity to endure stresses and strains.

He delivered me from my strong enemy, and from them which hated me: for they were too strong for me. They prevented me in the day of my calamity: but the Lord was my stay.

Psalm 18:17-18

There is a deep-seated need in all of us to sense purpose—even out of calamity. Out of this thirst for meaning is born the simplistic yet crucial prayer, "Why?"….

No matter how painful the quest, we will still search through the rubbish of broken dreams, broken promises, and twisted childhood issues looking for clues. We don't have to necessarily erase the cause of our pain; we mainly just want to find some reason or justification for the pain and discomfort.

All of us know what it means to be left alone. Whether through death, desertion, or even disagreement, we have all been left alone at times. We are sometimes disillusioned when we find out how easily people will leave us. Generally they leave us when we think that we need them.

The struggle truly begins not when men surround us, but rather when they forsake us. It is then that we begin to discover our own identity and self-worth!

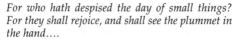

For who hath despised the day of small things?
For they shall rejoice, and shall see the plummet in
the hand....

Zechariah 4:10

I remember so well the early struggles that my wife and I had to maintain our family, finances, and overall well-being while building a ministry. I was working a secular job that God wanted me to leave for full-time ministry. Full-time ministry—what a joke! I was scarcely asked to preach anywhere that offered more than some food. Often I would preach until sweaty and tired, to rows of empty pews with two or three people who decorated the otherwise empty church.

Finally I said yes to full-time ministry. I did it not because I wanted it, but because the company I worked for went out of business and I was forced out of my comfort zone into the land of faith. What a frightening experience. I was without everything you could think of: without a job and then a car. I thought God had forgotten me. But I experienced more about God in those desperate days of struggle as I answered the charges of satan with the perseverance of prayer.

I know that the Lord will maintain the cause of the afflicted, and the right of the poor.

Psalm 140:12

It's hard for me as a man to fully understand how horrible rape is for women. I can sympathize, but the violation is incomprehensible. However, I have come to realize that rape is another creature inflicting his will on someone without her permission. Abuse is abnormal use. It is terrible to misuse or abuse anyone.

Many women feel guilty about things they had no control over. They feel guilty about being victimized. Often their original intention was to help another, but in the process they are damaged. Tamar was the king's daughter. She was a virgin. She was a "good girl." She didn't do anything immoral. It is amazing that her own brother would be so filled with desire that he would go to such lengths to destroy his sister. He thought he was in love. It wasn't love. It was lust. He craved her so intensely that he lost his appetite for food. He was visibly distorted with passion (see 2 Samuel 13). Love is a giving force, while lust is a selfish compulsion centralized on gratification.

Therefore we do not lose heart. Though outwardly we are wasting away, yet inwardly we are being renewed day by day. For our light and momentary troubles are achieving for us an eternal glory that far outweighs them all.

2 Corinthians 4:16-17 NIV

We went through a phase once when we thought real faith meant having no feelings. Although we don't want to be controlled by feelings, we must have access to our emotions. We need to allow ourselves the pleasure and pain of life.

Emotional pain is to the spirit what physical pain is to the body. Pain warns us that something is out of order and may require attention. Pain warns us that something in our body is not healed. When pain fills our heart, we know that we have an area where healing or restoration is needed. We dare not ignore these signals, and neither dare we let them control us.

We need to allow the Spirit of God to counsel us and guide us through the challenges of realignment when upheavals occur in our lives. Even the finest limousine requires a regular schedule of tune-ups or realignments. Minor adjustments increase performance and productivity.

Thou hast caused men to ride over our heads; we went through fire and through water: but Thou broughtest us out into a wealthy place.

Psalm 66:12

———•———

Satan cannot dispute your serving God, but he challenges our reason for serving Him. He says it is for the prominence and protection that God provides. He insinuates that if things weren't going so well, we would not praise God so fervently. In each of our lives, in one way or another, we will face times when we must answer satan's charges and prove that even in the storm, He is still God!

Times of challenge in my early ministry sorely tried all that was in me. If you can remember your beginnings and still reach toward your goals, God will bless you with things without fear of those items becoming idols in your life. There is a glory in the early years that people who didn't have to struggle seem not to possess. There is a strange sense of competence that comes from being born in the flames of struggle. How exuberant are the first steps of the child who earlier was mobile only through crawling on his hands and knees.

Deliver the poor and needy: rid them out of the hand of the wicked.

Psalm 82:4

The enemy wants to violate God's children. He is planning and plotting your destruction. He has watched you with wanton eyes. He has great passion and perseverance. Jesus told Peter, *"Satan hath desired to have you, that he may sift you as wheat: but I have prayed for thee..."* (Luke 22:31-32). Satan lusts after God's children. He wants you. He craves for you with an animalistic passion. He awaits an opportunity for attack. In addition, he loves to use people to fulfill the same kinds of lust upon one another.

Often the residual effects of being abused linger for many years. Some never find deliverance because they never allow Christ to come into the dark places of their life. Jesus has promised to set you free from every curse of the past. He wants the whole person well—in body, emotions, and spirit. He will deliver you from all the residue of your past. Perhaps the incident is over but the crippling is still there. He also will deal with the crippling that's left in your life.

*Consider it pure joy, my brothers, whenever you
face trials of many kinds, because you know that the
testing of your faith develops perseverance.*

James 1:2-3 NIV

In spite of the pain and distaste of adversity, it is impossible not to notice that each adverse event leaves sweet nectar behind, which, in turn, can produce its own rich honey in the character of the survivor. It is this bitter-sweet honey that allows us to enrich the lives of others through our experiences and testimonies. There is absolutely no substitute for the syrupy nectar of human experiences. It is these experiences that season the future relationships God has in store for us.

Unfortunately, many people leave their situation bitter and not better. Be careful to bring the richness of the experience to the hurting, not the unresolved bitterness. This kind of bitterness is a sign that the healing process in you is not over and, therefore, is not ready to be shared. You must come to a place of separation and decide to live on. When we have gone through the full cycle of survival, the situations and experiences in our lives will produce no pain, only peace.

Therefore thus saith the Lord God, Behold, I lay in Zion for a foundation a stone, a tried stone, a precious corner stone, a sure foundation: he that believeth shall not make haste.

Isaiah 28:16

I have found God to be a builder of men. When He builds, He emphasizes the foundation. A foundation, once it is laid, is neither visible nor attractive, but nevertheless still quite necessary. When God begins to establish the foundation, He does it in the feeble, frail beginnings of our lives. Paul describes himself as a wise master builder. Actually, God is the Master Builder. He knows what kind of beginning we need and He lays His foundation in the struggles of our formative years.

I don't think I completely realized how severe my early years of ministry were because I saw them through the tinted glasses of grace. I had been gifted with the grace to endure. Often we don't realize how severe our beginnings were until we are out or about to come out of them. Then the grace lifts and we behold the utter devastating truth about what we just came through.

*And this I pray, that your love may abound still
more and more in knowledge and all discernment.*
Philippians 1:9 NKJV

One of the things that makes many women particularly vulnerable to different types of abuse and manipulation is their maternal instinct. Wicked men frequently capitalize on this tendency in order to have their way with women. The gift of discernment must operate in your life.

The number of cases of violence within relationships and marriages is growing at an alarming rate. The incidence of date rape is reaching epidemic proportions. The fastest growing form of murder today is within relationships. Husbands and wives and girlfriends and boyfriends are killing one another. Often women have taken to murder in order to escape the constant violence of an abusive husband.

Another form of abuse is more subtle. There are men who often coerce women into a sexual relationship by claiming that they love them. It is a terrible feeling to be used by someone. He makes every kind of excuse possible for taking advantage of her, and she, because of her vulnerability, follows blindly along until the relationship has gone so far that she is trapped.

And He arose, and rebuked the wind, and said unto
the sea, Peace, be still. And the wind ceased, and
there was a great calm.

Mark 4:39

Have you allowed God to stand in the bow of your ship and speak peace to the thing that once terrified you? We can only benefit from resolved issues. The great tragedy is that most of us keep our pain active. Our power is never activated because our past remains unresolved. If we want to see God's power come from the pain of an experience, we must allow the process of healing to take us beyond bitterness into a resolution that releases us from the prison and sets us free.

To never trust again is to live on the pinnacle of a tower. You always talk about the past because you stopped living years ago. Listen to your speech. You discuss the past as if it were the present because the past has stolen the present right out of your hand! In the name of Jesus, get it back! God's healing process makes us free to taste life again, free to trust again, and free to live without threatening fears.

And I, brethren, could not speak unto you as unto spiritual, but as unto carnal, even as unto babes in Christ.

1 Corinthians 3:1

When I was very small, my family had a tradition we observed every Sunday breakfast. Every Sunday morning my mother would go into the kitchen while we were still asleep and begin making homemade waffles for breakfast. These were real waffles. I don't remember all the ingredients she had in them, but I do remember that this particular recipe required beating the egg whites and then folding them into the waffle batter.

They smelled like Hallelujah and they looked like glory to God—if you know what I mean. They took a long time to prepare, but these waffles took your mouth to the butter-filled streams of heaven.

The other day I tasted some of these modern carbon-copy, freezer burned, cardboard-clad waffles. My taste buds recoiled. My point is, I am afraid that too many Christians pop off the altar like these cardboard waffles. They are overnight wonders. They are 24-hour pastors with a Bible they haven't read and a briefcase more valuable than the sermons in it!

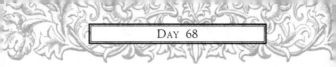

...For the Lord hath comforted His people, and will have mercy upon His afflicted.

Isaiah 49:13

Men who have sex with women without being committed to them are just as guilty of abuse as a rapist. A woman may have given her body to such a man, but she did so because of certain expectations. When someone uses another person for sex by misleading them, it is the same as physical rape. The abuse is more subtle, but it amounts to the same thing. Both the abuser and the victim are riding into a blazing inferno. Anything can happen when a victim has had enough.

Some women suffer from low self-esteem. They are victims and they don't even know it. Perhaps every time something goes wrong, you think it's your fault. It is not your fault if you are being abused in this way; it is your fault if you don't allow God's Word to arrest sin and weakness in your life. It is time to let go of every ungodly relationship. Do it now! There are those who attend church who are incestuous. It still happens today, but God is saying that enough is enough!

Be still, and know that I am God: I will be exalted among the heathen, I will be exalted in the earth.

Psalm 46:10

All too often, our thoughts and conversations reveal that we wrestle with characters who have moved on and events that don't really matter. The people who surround us are kept on hold while we invest massive amounts of attention to areas of the past that are dead and possess no ability to reward.

I think that the greatest of all depressions comes when we live and gather our successes just to prove something to someone who isn't even looking. God did most of His work on creation with no one around to applaud His accomplishments. So He praised Himself. He said, "It was good!"

Have you stopped to appreciate what God has allowed you to accomplish, or have you been too busy trying to make an impression on someone? Somewhere beyond loneliness there is contentment, and contentment is born out of necessity. It springs up in the heart that lives in an empty house, and in the smile that comes on the face of a person who has amused himself with his own thoughts.

But, beloved, be not ignorant of this one thing, that one day is with the Lord as a thousand years, and a thousand years as one day .

2 Peter 3:8

God takes His time developing us. A small beginning is just the prelude to a tremendous crescendo at the finale! Many of God's masterpieces were developed in small obscure circumstances. Moses, sent to the lost sheep of Israel, was trained in leadership while shoveling sheep dung on the backside of the desert. Granted, his discipline was developed in the royal courts of Pharaoh's house, but his disposition was shaped through failure and a desert kingdom with no one to lead but flies, gnats, and sheep. Who would have thought, looking at Moses' church of goat deacons and gnats for choir members, that he later would lead the greatest movement in the history of Old Testament theology?

You can't tell what's in you by looking at you. God is establishing patience, character, and concentration in the school of "nothing seems to be happening." Just because God promises to move in your life and anoints you to do a particular function doesn't mean that your foundation will be immediately built.

Now the God of hope fill you with all joy and peace in believing, that ye may abound in hope, through the power of the Holy Ghost.

Romans 15:13

———

The Lord is calling the hurting to Him. He will fill that void in your life. He wants to be that heavenly Father who will mend your heart with a positive role model. Through the Spirit, He wants to hold and nurture you. Millions have longed for a positive hug and nurturing embrace from fathers without ever receiving what they longed for.

Men, God is healing us so we can recognize that a woman who is not our wife is to be treated as our sister. Women must learn that they can have a platonic relationship with men. A brotherly and sisterly love does not include sexual intimacy. It does not include self-gratification.

Big brothers tend to protect their little sisters. They tend to watch for traps that may be placed in the sisters' way. Abused women have confused ideas abut relationships, and may not understand a healthy platonic relationship with the opposite sex. There is a way to fill that emptiness inside. It is through a relationship with God.

In whom also we have obtained an inheritance, being predestinated according to the purpose of Him who worketh all things after the counsel of His own will.

Ephesians 1:11

Have you reached that place in life where you enjoy your own company? Have you taken the time to enjoy your own personhood? When other people give affirmation, it reflects their opinion about you. When they leave, you may feel worthless and insignificant. But when you speak comfort and blessings to yourself, it reflects your own opinion about yourself. The best scenario is to enjoy both kinds of affirmation.

There are reasons to give yourself a standing ovation. The first is the fact that your steps are carefully observed and arranged by God Himself. They are designed to achieve a special purpose in your life. The Bible says, *"If God be for us, who can be against us?"* (Rom. 8:31b). So you must rejoice because you are in step with the beat of Heaven and the purposes of God. Second, you ought to rejoice because you are pursuing a goal that defies human manipulation. Your blessing rests in accomplishing the will of God.

Until we all reach unity in the faith and in the knowledge of the Son of God and become mature, attaining to the whole measure of the fullness of Christ.

Ephesians 4:13 NIV

Many misunderstand the prophecies of the Lord and so feel discontentment and despair. Just because God promises to move in your life and anoints you to do a particular function doesn't mean that your foundation will be immediately built. Joseph received a dream from the Lord that showed him ruling and reigning over his brothers, but in the next event his brothers stripped him, beat him, and tossed him in a hole...a dark hole of small beginnings.

Don't die in the hole! God hasn't changed His mind. He is a Master Builder and He spends extra time laying a great foundation.

When the first man Adam was created, he was created full grown. He had no childhood, no small things. But when it was time for the last man Adam, God didn't create Him full grown. No, He took His time and laid a foundation. He was born a child and laid in a manger. Please allow yourself time to grow.

Let your light so shine before men, that they may see your good works, and glorify your Father which is in heaven.

Matthew 5:17

It is wonderful to have a plan, but that means nothing if you have no power to perform the plan and accomplish the purpose. God sends people in and out of your life to exercise your faith and develop your character. When they are gone, they leave you with the reality that your God is with you to deliver you wherever you go! Moses died and left Joshua in charge, but God told him, *"As I was with Moses, so I will be with thee"* (Josh. 1:5). Joshua never would have learned that while Moses was there. You learn this kind of thing when "Moses" is gone. Power is developed in the absence of human assistance. Then we can test the limits of our resourcefulness and the magnitude of the favor of God.

There is within the most timid person—beneath that soft, flaccid demeanor—a God-given strength that supercedes any weakness he appeared to have. The Bible puts it this way: *"I can do all things through Christ which strengtheneth me"* (Phil. 4:13)!

By this shall all men know that ye are My disciples,
if ye have love one to another.

John 13:35

Society often places a woman's worth on her sexual appeal. Nothing is further from the truth. Self-esteem cannot be earned by performance in bed. Society suggests that the only thing men want is sex. Men, in general, are not the enemy. Draw a line of demarcation and say to yourself, "That was then and this is now!"

God's people are to nurture and protect one another. It makes no difference how tempestuous our past life has been. Even in the face of abuse, God still cares. Allow God the privilege of taking you in. *"He that dwelleth in the secret place of the most High shall abide under the shadow of the Almighty"* (Ps. 91:1).

Did you know that God has intensive care? He will take you in His arms. That love of God is flowing into broken lives all over the country. Don't believe for one moment that no one cares; God cares and the Church is learning to become a conduit of that concern. At last, we are in the school of love.

For even Christ did not please Himself; but as it is written, "The reproaches of those who reproached You fell on Me."

Romans 15:3 NKJV

Buried deep within the broken heart is a vital need to release and resolve. Although we feel pain when we fail at any task, there is a sweet resolve that delivers us from the cold clutches of uncertainty. If we had not been through some degree of rejection, we would have never been selected by God. Do you realize that God chooses people that others reject?! From a rejected son like David to a nearly murdered son like Joseph, God gathers the castaways of men and recycles them for Kingdom building.

What frustration exists in the lives of people who want to be used of God, but who cannot endure rejection from men. I haven't always possessed the personality profile that calloused me and offered some protection from the backlash of public opinion. If you want to be tenacious, you must be able to walk in the light of God's selection rather than dwell in the darkness of people's rejection. These critics are usually just a part of God's purpose in your life.

And the winds blew, and beat upon that house;
and it fell: and great was the fall of it.

Matthew 7:27

Once I was praying for the Lord to move mightily in my ministry. The Lord answered my prayer by saying, "You are concerned about building a ministry, but I am concerned about building a man." He gave a warning, which has echoed throughout my life. He said, "Woe unto the man whose ministry becomes bigger than he is!" Since then I have concerned myself with praying for the minister and not for the ministry. I realized that if the house outgrows the foundation, gradually the foundation will crack, the walls will collapse, and great will be the fall of it! No matter what you are trying to build, whether it is a business, a ministry, or a relationship, give it time to grow.

Humility is a necessity when you know that every accomplishment had to be the result of the wise Master Builder who knows when to do what. He knew when I needed friends. I trust Him more dearly and more nearly than I have ever trusted Him before. He is too wise to make a mistake!

The stone which the builders rejected, the same is become the head of the corner: this is the Lord's doing, and it is marvelous in our eyes?

Matthew 21:42b

Jesus concluded that the rejections of men He experienced were the doings of the Lord! The Lord orchestrates what the enemy does and makes it accomplish His purpose in your life. If I hadn't faced trials, I wouldn't have been ready for the blessings I now enjoy.

In the hands of God, even our most painful circumstances become marvelous in our eyes! However, rejection is only marvelous in the eyes of someone whose heart has wholly trusted in the Lord! Do you trust in the Lord, or are you grieving over something that someone has done—as though you have no God to direct it and no grace to correct it?

This question challenges the perspectives you have chosen to take for your life. *"It is marvelous in our eyes"* simply means that from our perspective, the worst things look good!

Faith is not needed just to remove problems; it is also needed to endure problems that seem immovable. Even if God didn't move it, He is able!

Bear ye one another's burdens, and so fulfil the law of Christ.

Galatians 6:2

L ove embraces the totality of the other person. It is impossible to completely and effectively love someone without being included in that other person's history. Our history has made us who we are. The images, scars, and victories that we live with have shaped us into the people we have become. We will never know who a person is until we understand where they have been.

The secret of being transformed from a vulnerable victim to a victorious, loving person is found in the ability to open your past to someone responsible enough to share your weaknesses and pains. You don't have to keep reliving it. You can release it. We are all in this walk together, and therefore can build one another up and carry some of the load with which our sisters are burdened.

There is hope for victims. There is no need to feel weak when one has Jesus Christ. His power is enough to bring about the kinds of changes that will set you free. He is calling, through the work of the Holy Spirit, for you to be set free.

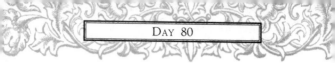

*But to those who do not believe, "The stone the
builders rejected has become the capstone...."*

1 Peter 2:7 NIV

Normally, anytime there is a crash, there is an injury. In the same way, a crashing relationship affects everyone associated with it, whether it is in a corporate office, a ministry, or a family. What is important is the fact that we don't have to die in the crashes and collisions of life. We must learn to live life with a seat belt in place, even though it is annoying to wear. Similarly, we need spiritual and emotional seat belts as well. We don't need the kind that harness us in and make us live like a mannequin; rather, we need the kind that are invisible, but greatly appreciated in a crash.

Inner assurance is the seat belt that stops you from going through the roof when you are rejected. It is inner assurance that holds you in place. It is the assurance that God is in control and that what He has determined no one can disallow! Praise God, for He will use the cornerstone developed through rejections and failed relationships to perfect what He has prepared!

Not that I speak in respect of want: for I have learned, in whatsoever state I am, therewith to be content. I know both how to be abased, and I know how to abound:

Philippians 4:11

If you are praying, "Lord, make me bigger," you are probably miserable, although prayerful. Did you know you can be prayerful and still be miserable? Anytime you use prayer to change God, who is perfect, instead of using prayer to change yourself, you are miserable. Instead, try praying this: "Lord, make me better." I admit that better is harder to measure and not as noticeable to the eye. But better will overcome bigger every time.

What a joy it is to be at peace with who you are and where you are in your life. I want to be better—to have a better character, better confidence, and a better attitude! The desire to be bigger will not allow you to rest, relax, or enjoy your blessing. The desire to be better, however, will afford you a barefoot stroll down a deserted beach. Thank God for the things that you know He brought you through. Thank God for small things.

Hear counsel, and receive instruction, that thou mayest be wise in the latter end.

Proverbs 19:20

This morning when I rose, I watched the miracle of beginnings from the veranda of my hotel. Far to the east the sun crept up on stage as if it was trying to arrive without disturbing anyone. It peeked up over the ocean like the eye of a child around a corner as he stealthily plays peek-a-boo.

If I had not stayed perched on my window's edge, I would have misjudged the day. I would have thought that the morning or perhaps the sun-drenched afternoon was the most beautiful part of the day. But just before I turned in my ballot and cast my vote, the evening slipped up on the stage. I looked over in the distance as the sun began its descent. I noticed that the crescendo of the concert is always reserved for the closing. The sun had changed her sundress to an evening gown, full of color and grandeur. The grace of a closing day is far greater than the uncertainty of morning. The most beautiful part of a woman's life, is at the setting of the sun.

*For you know that we dealt with each of you as a
father deals with his own children, encouraging,
comforting and urging you to live lives worthy of
God, who calls you into His kingdom and glory.*

1 Thessalonians 2:11-12 NIV

Isn't it amazing how we can see so much potential in
others, yet find it difficult to unlock our own hidden
treasure? Nurturing is the investment necessary to stim-
ulate the potential that we possess. Without nurturing,
inner strengths may remain dormant. Therefore it is crucial to our development that there be some degree of
nurturing the intrinsic resources we possess.

There is a difference in the emotional makeup of a child
who has had a substantial deposit of affection and affirmation. Great affirmation occurs when someone invests
into our personhood. Anyone will invest in a sure success,
but aren't we grateful when someone supports us when
we were somewhat of a risk?

Unfortunately, nothing brings luster to your character
and commitment to your heart like opposition does.
The finished product is a result of the fiery process. It
creates someone who shines with the kind of brilliancy
that enables God to look down and see Himself.

To every thing there is a season, and a time to every purpose under the heaven.

Ecclesiastes 31:1

————

I write this with my mother in mind. Her hair has changed colors before my eyes. Lines are etched upon her brow. Her arms are weaker now and her gait much slower; but she is somehow warmer at life's winter age than she was in the summer days. All of life's tragedy has been wrestled to the mat and still she stands to attest to the authenticity of her goals, dreams, and ambitions.

What is wrong with collecting an encore from a grateful audience whose lives have been touched by your song? Just because the glare of summer doesn't beat upon your face doesn't mean that there is nothing left for you to do.

Whose presence will stand as a witness that God will see you through? God never extends days beyond purpose. My daughters are in their springtime, my wife is in the middle of summer, and my mother is walking through autumn to step into winter. Together they form a chord of womanhood—three different notes creating a harmonious blend. To the reader, I would suggest: Enjoy every note.

Am I a God at hand, saith the Lord, and not a God far off? Can any hide himself in secret places that I shall not see him? saith the Lord. Do not I fill heaven and earth? saith the Lord.

Jeremiah 23:23-24

There is no tiptoeing around the presence of God with pristine daintiness—as if we could tiptoe softly enough not to awaken a God who never sleeps nor slumbers. We shuffle in His presence like children who were instructed not to disturb their Father, although God isn't sleepy and He doesn't have to go to work. He is alive and awake, and He is well.

It is the nature of a fallen man to hide from God. If you will remember, Adam also hid from God. How ridiculous it is for us to think that we can hide from Him! His intelligence supercedes our frail ability to be deceptive. When a man hides himself from God, he loses himself. What good is it to know where everything else is, if we cannot find ourselves? Our loss causes a desperation that produces sin and separation. We need to become transparent in the presence of the Lord.

Now she that is a widow indeed, and desolate, trusteth in God, and continueth in supplication and prayers night and day.

1 Timothy 5:5

It is important that we teach women to prepare for the winter. I believe age can be stressful for women in a way that it isn't for men—only because we have not historically recognized women at other stages in their lives. Equally disturbing is the fact that statisticians tell us women tend to live longer, more productive lives than their male counterparts. Because of an early death of their spouse, they have no sense of companionship.

The Bible admonishes us to minister to the widows. We need to invest some effort in encouraging older women. They have a need for more than just provision of natural substance. Many women spend their lives building their identity around their role rather than around their person. When the role changes, they feel somewhat displaced. When circumstances change, older women can feel unfulfilled. Don't allow changing times to change who you are. Do not lose your identity in your circumstances. Maintain a sense of worth. Redefine your purpose, gather your assets and keep on living and giving.

...for He is like a refiner's fire, and like fuller's soap.
Malachi 3:2b

God places His prize possessions in the fire. The precious vessels that He draws the most brilliant glory from often are exposed to the melting pot of distress. The bad news is, even those who live godly lives will suffer persecution. The good news is, you might be in the fire, but God controls the thermostat! He knows how hot it needs to be to accomplish His purpose in your life. I don't know anyone I would rather trust with the thermostat than the God of all grace.

Every test has degrees. Some people have experienced similar distresses, but to varying degrees. God knows the temperature that will burn away the impurities from His purpose. He has had to fan the flames to produce the effects that He wanted in my life. God is serious about producing the change in us that will glorify Him.

His hand has fanned the flames that were needed to teach patience, prayer, and many other invaluable lessons. We need His corrections. We don't enjoy them, but we need them. He affirms our position in Him by correcting and chastening us.

Trust in the Lord with all thine heart; and lean not unto thine own understanding. In all thy ways acknowledge Him, and He shall direct thy paths.

Proverbs 3:5-6

Discouragement comes when people feel they have seen it all and most of it was really terrible! No matter what age you are, you have never seen it all. There are no graduations from the school of life other than death. No one knows how God will end His book, but He does tend to save the best for last. Israel didn't recognize Jesus because they were so used to seeing what they had already seen. God had sent dozens of prophets, and when He finally sends a king, they failed to recognize Him.

It is dangerous to assume that what you will see out of life will be similar to what you saw before. God has the strangest way of restoring purpose to your life. For Naomi, it was through a relationship she tried to dissuade. It is dangerous to keep sending people away. The very one you are trying to send away may have the key to restoring purpose and fulfillment to your life.

Let us therefore come boldly unto the throne of grace, that we may obtain mercy, and find grace to help in time of need.

Hebrews 4:16

Why would Adam, a lost man, cover himself with leaves? Adam said, "I was afraid." Fear separated this son from his Father; fear caused him to conspire to deceive his only Solution. This fear was not reverence. It was desperation.

If Adam had only run toward instead of away from God, he could have been delivered! Why then do we continue to present a God who cannot be approached to a dying world? Many in the Christian family are still uncomfortable with their heavenly Father. Some Christians do not feel accepted in the beloved. They feel that their relationship with God is meritorious, but they are intimidated because of His holiness. His holiness exposes our flaws. Yet His grace allows us to approach Him—though we are not worthy—through the bloody skins soaked with Christ's blood.

Who else knows you like God does? If you hide from His perfect love, you will never be able to enjoy a relationship with your heavenly Father and be comfortable enough to sit in His lap.

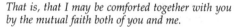

*That is, that I may be comforted together with you
by the mutual faith both of you and me.*

Romans 1:12

Ruth was Naomi's daughter-in-law. Naomi thought their only connection was her now dead son. Many times we, who have been very family-oriented, do not understand friendships. When family circumstances change, we lapse into isolation because we know nothing of other relationships.

There are bonds that are stronger than blood. They are God-bonds! When God brings someone into our life, He is the bonding agent. Ruth said, "Your God shall be my God." God wanted Naomi to see the splendor of winter relationships, the joy of passing the baton of her wisdom and strength to someone worthy of her attention. Let God choose such a person for us because too often we choose on the basis of fleshly ties and not godly ties.

Ruth would have died in Moab, probably marrying some heathenistic idolator if it were not for the wisdom of Naomi, an older, more seasoned woman. Naomi knew how to provide guidance without manipulation—a strength many women at that stage of life do not have. Ruth had greatness in her that God used Naomi to cultivate.

Verily, verily, I say unto you, Except a corn of wheat fall into the ground and die, it abideth alone: but if it die, it bringeth forth much fruit.

John 12:24

It is impossible to discuss the value of investing in people and not find ourselves worshiping God—what a perfect picture of investment. God is the major stockholder. No matter who He later uses to enhance our characters, we need to remember the magnitude of God's investment in our lives. The greatest primary investment He made was the inflated, unthinkable price of redemption that He paid. No one else would have bought us at that price. He paid the ultimate price when He died for our sins.

God has an investment in our lives. First of all, no one invests without the expectation of gain. What would a perfect God have to gain from investing in an imperfect man? According to Scripture, we possess treasure. However, the excellency of what we have is not of us, but of God. The treasure is "of" God. This treasure originates from God. It is accumulated in us and then presented back to Him. Your inheritance is encased in your treasure.

Likewise, teach the older women to be reverent in the way they live… Then they can train the younger women to love their husbands and children.

Titus 2:3-4 NIV

Elisabeth, the wife of the priest Zacharias, was a winter woman with a summer experience. She was pregnant with a promise. In spite of her declining years, she was fulfilling more destiny then than she had in her youth. She is biblical proof that God blesses us in His own time and on His own terms. She was a recluse for six months until she heard a knock at the door. If you have isolated yourself from others, regardless of the reason, I pray you will hear the knocking of the Lord.

Opening the door changed Elisabeth's life forever. As you open the door to new relationships, God will overwhelm you with new splendor. Mary, the future mother of our Savior and Lord, Elisabeth's cousin, was at the door. The baby in Elisabeth's womb leap and Elisabeth was filled with the Holy Ghost. God will jump-start your heart! He doesn't mean for you to go sit in a chair and die! In Jesus' name, get up and answer the door!

I will say of the Lord, He is my refuge and my fortress: my God: in Him will I trust.

Psalm 91:2

The basis of any relationship must be trust. Trusting God with your successes isn't really a challenge. The real test of trust is to be able to share your secrets, your inner failures and fears. A mutual enhancement comes into a relationship where there is intimacy based on honesty.

We have nothing to fear, for our honesty with the Father doesn't reveal anything to Him that He doesn't already know! He knows of your failure before you fail. His knowledge is all-inclusive. He knows our thoughts even as we unconsciously gather them together to make sense in our own mind!

Once we know this, all our attempts at silence and secrecy seem juvenile and ridiculous. When we pray, and more importantly, when we commune with God, we must have the kind of confidence and assurance that neither requires nor allows deceit. His love is incomprehensible, because there is nothing with which we can compare it! What we must do is accept the riches of His grace and stand in the shade of His loving arms.

For I will restore health unto thee, and I will heal thee of thy wounds, saith the Lord.

Jeremiah 30:17a

It takes patience to overcome the effects of years of use and abuse. If you are not committed to getting back what you once had, you could easily decide that the process is impossible. Nevertheless, I assure you it is not impossible. David, the psalmist, declares, *"He restoreth my soul"* (Ps. 23:3). The term restoreth is a process. Only God knows what it takes to remove the build-up that may exist in your life.

Prejudice is to pre-judge. People, even believers, have often prejudged God. However, He isn't finished yet. Therefore, you are not off course. Trust Him to see you through days that may be different from the ones you encountered earlier. You are being challenged with the silent struggles of winter. I believe the most painful experience is to look backward and have to stare into the cold face of regret. First pause and thank God that, in spite of the tragedies of youth, it is a miracle that you survived the solemn chill of former days. Your presence should be a praise.

But He knoweth the way that I take: When He hath tried me, I shall come forth as gold.

Job 23:10

We spend most of our time talking about what we want from God. The real issue is what He wants from us. It is the Lord who has the greatest investment. We are the parched, dry ground from which Christ springs. Believe me, God is serious about His investment!

God will fight to protect the investment He has placed in your life. What a comfort it is to know that the Lord has a vested interest in my deliverance. God has begun the necessary process of cultivating what He has invested in my life. Have you ever stopped to think that it was God's divine purpose that kept you afloat when others capsized beneath the load of life? Look at Job; he knew that God had an investment in his life that no season of distress could eradicate.

Have you ever gone through a dilemma that should have scorched every area of your life and yet you survived the pressure? Then you ought to know that He is Lord over the fire!

*Therefore the redeemed of the Lord shall return, and
come with singing unto Zion; and everlasting joy
shall be upon their head: they shall obtain gladness
and joy; and sorrow and mourning shall flee away.*
Isaiah 51:11

There is one thing every Naomi can rely upon as she
gathers wood for winter days and wraps quilts
around weak, willowy legs: God is a restorer. That is to
say, as you sit by the fire sipping coffee, rehearsing your
own thoughts, playing old reruns from the scenes in
your life—some things He will explain and others He
will heal.

Restoration doesn't mean all the lost people who left you
will return. Neither Naomi's husband nor her sons were
resurrected. It is just that God gives purpose back to the
years that had question marks. Simply said, "He'll make
it up to you." He restores the effects of the years of tur-
moil. People who heard Naomi complaining that God
had dealt bitterly, should have waited as God masterfully
brought peace into her arms. The smile on her leathery
face and the calmness of her rest says, *"He doeth all
things well"* (see Mark 7:37).

Likewise the Spirit also helpeth our infirmities: for we know not what we should pray for as we ought: but the Spirit itself maketh intercession for us with groanings which cannot be uttered.

Romans 8:26

One thing we search for at every level of our relationships is "to be understood." When I am properly understood, I don't always have to express and explain. Thank You, Lord, for not asking me to explain what I oft can scarcely express!

We quickly grow weary when we are around anyone who demands that we constantly qualify our statements and explain our intent. But God clearly perceives and understands our every need.

We are to live in a state of open communication with God, not necessarily jabbering at Him nonstop for hours. Many people end up watching the clock while they utter mindless rhetoric, trying to get in the specified amount of time in prayer.

We don't need to labor to create what is already there. I am glad my Savior knows what my speech and my silence suggest. I need not labor to create what we already share in the secret place of our hearts!

Inasmuch as ye have done it unto one of the least of these My brethren, ye have done it unto Me.

Matthew 25:40b

There is something every person can rely on during their winter season of life. The Lord will be known as: the nourisher. You, who have been the source for others to be strengthened, may find it difficult to know what to do with this role reversal. The nourisher must learn to be nourished. Many women pray more earnestly as intercessors for others than for themselves. That is wonderful, but there ought to be a time that you desire certain things for yourself. Our God is El Shaddai, giving strength to the feeble and warmth to the cold. There is comfort in His arms. Like children, even adults can snuggle into His everlasting arms and hear the heartbeat of a loving God.

Expect God in all His varied forms. He is a master of disguise, a guiding star in the night, a lily left growing in the valley, or an answered prayer sent on the breath of an angel. God can use anyone as a channel of nourishment. Regardless of the channel, He is still the source.

When thou passest through the waters, I will be with thee; and through the rivers, they shall not overflow thee: when thou walkest through the fire, thou shalt not be burned; neither shall the flame kindle upon thee.

Isaiah 43:2

It has been suggested that if you walk in the Spirit, you won't have to contend with the fire. Real faith doesn't mean you won't go through the fire. The presence of the Lord can turn a burning inferno into a walk in the park! The Bible says a fourth person was in the fire, and the three Hebrews were able to walk around unharmed in it (see Dan. 3).

King Nebuchadnezzar was astonished when he saw them overcome what had destroyed other men. I cannot guarantee that you will not face terrifying situations if you believe God. I can declare that if you face them with Christ's presence, the effects of the circumstance will be drastically altered. If you believe God, you can walk in what other men burn in. Seldom will anyone fully appreciate the fire you have walked through, but God knows the fiery path to accomplishment. He can heal the blistered feet of the traveler.

And in the sixth month the angel Gabriel was sent from God unto a city of Galilee, named Nazareth, to a virgin espoused to a man whose name was Joseph, of the house of David; and the virgin's name was Mary.

Luke 1:26-27

…What aileth thee, Hagar?… Arise, lift up the lad, and hold him in thine hand; for I will make him a great nation.

Genesis 21:17-18

When Hagar was lost in the wilderness of depression and wrestling exasperation, God sent an angel. When the labor-ridden mother of Samson was mundane and barren, God sent an angel. When young Mary was wandering listlessly through life, God sent an angel. When the grief-stricken Mary Magdalene came stumbling down to the tomb, God sent an angel. For every woman in crises, there is an angel! For every lonely night and forgotten mother, there is an angel. For every lost young girl wandering the concrete jungle of an inner city, there is an angel. My sister, set your coffee down, take the blanket off your legs, and stand up on your feet! Hast thou not known, hast thou not heard? For every woman facing winter, there is an angel!

Neither is there any creature that is not manifest in His sight: but all things are naked and opened unto the eyes of Him with whom we have to do.

Hebrews 4:13

We are called to live in a state of openhearted communication with the Lord. Yes, we feel vulnerable when we realize that our hearts are completely exposed before God. Yet every one of us desperately needs to have someone who is able to help us, someone who is able to understand the issues that are etched on the tablets of our heart!

Since we already feel exposed when we realize that there is not one thought we have entertained that God has not seen and heard, then there is no need for a sanctimonious misrepresentation of who we are! We no longer need to live under the strain of continual camouflage. We are naked before Him, just as a man sprawls naked on the operating table before a surgeon. The man is neither boastful nor embarrassed, for he understands that his exposed condition is a necessity. We need to show God what is hindering His flow of life to us so He can clean us.

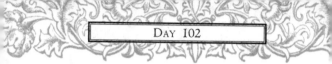

Being confident of this very thing, that He which hath begun a good work in you will perform it until the day of Jesus Christ.

Philippians 1:6

I think it would be remiss of me not to share, before moving on, the miracles of winter. In the summer, all was well with Sarah. At that time she knew little about Jehovah, her husband's God. She basically knew she was in love with a wonderful man.

Soon the giddy exuberance of summer started to ebb as she began wrestling with the harsh realities of following a dreamer. What was really troubling her was the absence of a child. By now she was sure she was barren. She felt like she had cheated Abraham out of an important part of life. Someone had said she would have a baby. Sarah laughed, "If I am going to get a miracle, God had better hurry." I want to warn you against setting your own watch. God's time is not your time. He may not come when you want Him to, but He is right on time. After she had gone through life's experiences, she learned that God is faithful to perform His Word.

*...when thou walkest through the fire, thou shalt not
be burned; neither shall the flame kindle upon thee.*

Isaiah 43:2b

Your Deliverer knows what it feels like to be in the
fire. Thank God for running swiftly to meet His
children in the fire of affliction and need. But still the
question remains, "Is there any preventive protection
that will at least aid the victim who struggles in the
throes of a fiery test?" If you are in a fiery trial, be
advised that it is your faith that is on trial. If you are to
overcome the dilemma, it will not be by your feelings,
but by your faith.

First John 5:4 says, *"For whatsoever is born of God
overcometh the world: and this is the victory that overcometh the world, even our faith."* Yes, it is the shield of
faith that quenches the fiery darts of the devil (see Eph.
6:16). The term quench means "to extinguish." Are there
any fires brewing that you would like to extinguish? Your
faith will do the job. If faith doesn't deliver you from it,
then it will surely deliver you through it.

Now no chastening for the present seemeth to be joyous, but grievous: nevertheless afterward it yieldest the peaceable fruit of righteousness unto them which are exercised thereby....

Hebrews 12:11-12

THE FIRST LAUGH—The Laugh of Unbelief

Abraham and Sarah were already old and well advanced in years, and Sarah was past the age of childbearing. So Sarah laughed to herself as she thought, "After I am worn out and my master is old, will I now have this pleasure?" Then the Lord said to Abraham, "Why did Sarah laugh and say, 'Will I really have a child, now that I am old?' Is anything too hard for the Lord? I will return to you at the appointed time next year and Sarah will have a son" (Genesis 18:11-14 NIV).

THE LAST LAUGH—The Laugh of a Miracle

Sarah became pregnant and bore a son to Abraham in his old age, at the very time God had promised him. Abraham gave the name Isaac to the son Sarah bore. Abraham was a hundred years old when Isaac was born. Sarah said, "God has brought me laughter, and everyone who hears about this will laugh with me" (Genesis 21:2-6 NIV).

Come now; and let us reason together, saith the Lord: though your sins be as scarlet, they shall be whiter as snow; though they be red like crimson, they shall be as wool.

Isaiah 1:18

The slate has been cleansed at Calvary, but the mind is being renewed from day to day. As images came from time to time with flashbacks of things that haunted my mind like ghosts unexorcised, I began to seek the Lord who saved me for the grace to keep me. It was then that I began to realize the great truth that the blood of Christ doesn't just reach backward into the bleakness of my past debauchery—it also has the power to cover my ongoing struggles!

The blood of Christ covers my past, present, and future struggles—not so I could run through my inheritance like the prodigal son, but so I might have a comfort as I lie on the table of His grace. I must relax in this comfort and assurance and allow the tools of day-to-day tests and struggles to skillfully implant into my heart and mind a clearer reflection of His divine nature in me.

The fear of the Lord tendeth to life: and he that hath it shall abide satisfied; he shall not be visited with evil.

Proverbs 19:23

Between the announcement that Sarah would bear a child and when she gave birth, everything in her was tested.

Sarah followed Abraham out of their country and away from their kindred. Later, she takes another pilgrimage into what could have been a great tragedy. Abraham leads his wife into Gerar. As I am a man and a leader myself, I dare not be too hard on him. Anyone can make a poor decision. The decision to go to Gerar I could defend, even though Gerar means "halting place." I have made decisions that brought me to a halting place in my life. What's reprehensible is that Abraham, Sarah's protector and covering, when afraid for his own safety, lied about her identity (see Gen. 20). You never know who people are until you witness them under pressure. Abraham had a flagrant disregard for truth. And it was a life-threatening lie.

Sarah's love for Abraham gave her the courage to leave home, but her love for God brought forth the promised seed.

*From that time on Jesus began to explain to His
disciples that He must go to Jerusalem and suffer
many things at the hands of the elders, chief priests
and teachers of the law, and that He must be killed
and on the third day be raised to life....*

Matthew 16:21-23 NIV

Faith is a key issue for Christians that the people of the
early Church were simply called believers in recogni-
tion of their great faith. We need to understand the distinctions of faith. Faith cannot alter purpose; it only acts
as an agent to assist in fulfilling the predetermined purpose of God. Faith becomes the vehicle that enables us to
persevere and delivers us through the test. Faith guards
the purpose of God. It will deliver us out of the hand of
the enemy—the enemy being anything that hinders the
purpose of God in our lives.

Hebrews chapter 11 discusses the definition of faith. It
then shares the deeds of faith in verses 32-35a, and
finally it discusses the perseverance of faith in verses
35b-39. There are distinctions of faith as well. Hebrews
11:32-35a emphasizes the distinct faith that escapes peril
and overcomes obstacles.

*Who will not suffer you to be tempted above that
ye are able; but will with the temptation also make
a way to escape, that ye may be able to bear it.*

1 Corinthians 10:13

Have you ever known someone upon whom you had
cast the weight of your confidence, only to have
your trust defrauded in a moment of self-gratification
and indulgence? Someone who has a selfish need can
jeopardize all that you have.

Abraham's lie jeopardized the safety of his wife. King
Abimelech was a heathen king. He was used to getting
whatever he wanted. His reputation for debauchery pre-
ceded him so that Abraham, the father of faith, feared for
his life. Rather than risk himself, he told the king that his
wife was really his sister. Abraham knew that this would
cause Sarah to have to fulfill the torrid desires of a hea-
thenist. Her Abraham failed her. But God did not!

Maybe there is someone in your life who selfishly threw
you into a tempestuous situation. Take courage! Just
because satan has set a snare doesn't mean you can't
escape. The God we serve is able. His Word to you is,
"Woman, thou art loosed."

And he raised us up with Christ and gave us a seat with Him in the heavens. He did this for those in Christ Jesus so that for all future time He could show the very great riches of His grace by being kind to us in Christ Jesus.

Ephesians 2:6-7 NCV

I appreciate the peace that comes from knowing I am His child. I am His—even when I feel like a mess, even when I am embarrassed, for His grace is sufficient for me. I thank Him for the peace He gives to every believer who matures into a trust-filled relationship with Jesus Christ. My initial surgery may be completed, but daily I remain under His intensive care as He monitors my progressions and occasional digressions. I wouldn't trust my future with anybody but Him.

You will never worship God correctly if you live in the shadows, wrestling with unconfessed sin. Whatever you do, there is an ever-increasing need for you to find a place of comfort in the presence of the Lord. It is possible to escape my presence, but not His. He is ever present, waiting on you to stand before Him and be healed.

The Lord is at hand. Be careful for nothing; but in every thing by prayer and supplication with thanksgiving let your requests be made known unto God.

Philippians 4:5b-6

Abraham's faith had always been the star of the Old Testament, but not that day. It's amazing how faith will come up in your heart at a crisis. Abraham passed off Sarah as his sister to King Abimelech, knowing she would become part of the royal harem.

Consider Sarah. She is facing the anxious footsteps of her rapist. She knows it will not be long until she will be abused. Like a frightened rabbit, she realizes Abraham will not rescue her. I don't know what she prayed, but I know she cried out to the only One she had left! Maybe she said, "God of Abraham, I need you to be my God too. Save me from this pending fate." Or maybe she cried, "O God! Have mercy on me!" Whatever she said, God heard her.

He will hear you as well. You don't have time to be angry or bitter. You've just got enough time to pray. Call out to Him. He is your God too!

Yea doubtless, and I count all things but loss for the excellency of the knowledge of Christ Jesus my Lord: for whom I have suffered the loss of all things, and do count them but dung, that I may win Christ...that I may know Him....

Philippians 3:8-10

There are times in our lives when God will take us from one realm of faith to another. Christ knows what kind of heat to place upon us to produce the faith needed in the situation. When we present our bodies as living sacrifices, He is the God who answers by fire. The good news lies in the fact that when our faith collapses beneath the weight of unbelievable circumstances, He gives us His faith to continue on....

As the fire of persecution forces us to make deeper levels of commitment, our faith needs to be renewed to match our level of commitment. There is a place in God where the fire consumes every other desire but to know the Lord in the power of His resurrection. All other pursuits tarnish and seem worthless in comparison. Perhaps this is what Paul really pressed toward, that place of total surrender.

It is a good thing to give thanks unto the Lord, and to sing praises unto Thy name, O most High: to show forth Thy lovingkindness in the morning, and Thy faithfulness every night.

Psalm 92:1-2

"*For Sarah conceived, and bare Abraham a son in his old age, at the set time of which God had spoken to him*" (Genesis 21:2). It wasn't Abraham's visit to the tent that left that woman filled with the promise of God. Without God he could do nothing. Remember that man may be the instrument, but God is the life source. It was God who visited Sarah.

When Hebrews chapter 11 lists the patriarchs and their awesome faith, this winter woman's name is included. Abraham is mentioned for the kind of faith that would leave home and look for a city whose builder and maker is God (v. 10). But when it comes to discussing the kind of faith that caused an old woman's barren womb to conceive, it was Sarah's faith that did it. She just went through her winter clutching the warm hand of a loving God who would not fail. She understands the miracles that come only to winter women.

For he hath regarded the low estate of His hand-maiden: for, behold, from henceforth all generations shall call me blessed.

Luke 1:48

I believe it is important that women get healed and released in their spirits. I believe that God will move freshly in the lives of women in an even greater way.

God knows how to take a mess and turn it into a miracle. If you're in a mess, don't be too upset about it because God specializes in fixing messes. God is saying some definite things about women being set free and delivered to fulfill their purpose in the Kingdom.

When the Lord gets through working on you, all your adversaries will be ashamed. The people who contributed to your sense of low self-esteem will be ashamed when God gets through unleashing you. You won't have to prove anything. God will prove it. He will do it in your life. When He gets through showing that you've done the right thing and come to the right place, they will drop their heads and be ashamed.

If you have a past that torments you, Jesus can set you free. He will unleash your potential.

Not that we are sufficient of ourselves to think any thing as of ourselves; but our sufficiency is of God; who also hath made us able ministers of the new testament....

2 Corinthians 3:5-6

Time has hidden the future of a baby deeply within the tiny hands that someday will be different things to different people. "Who is this child?" the parents ponder. "When we are old, who will this child be? What is the level of contribution we have given to this world?" Time listens quietly, but still offers no answer.

The haunting question dulls with time, but still hums beneath the mind of the mature. "Who am I?" We have a deep need to find an answer. We are very interested in ourselves. Many of us come to know the Lord because we desperately need to know ourselves. Does that seem strange? It isn't, really. If we have a problem with an appliance, we always refer to an owner's manual. In our case it's the Bible. When repairs are needed, we go to the Manufacturer. Psalm 100 says, *"It is He that hath made us, and not we ourselves"* (Ps. 100:3b).

*But I am poor and needy; yet the Lord thinketh
upon me: Thou art my help and my deliverer; make
no tarrying, O my God.*

Psalm 40:17

Can you imagine how hard life was for the infirm
woman who was bowed over? (See Luke 13.) She
had to struggle, because of her problem, to come to
Jesus. Few of us are crippled in the same way. However,
we all face crippling limitations. We can be bowed over
financially. We can be bowed over emotionally. We can
be bowed over where we have no self-esteem. He wants
to see us struggling toward Him. Jesus could have
walked to this woman, but He chose not to. He wants to
see us struggle toward Him.

He wants you to want Him enough to overcome obstacles and to push in His direction. He doesn't want to just
throw things at you that you don't have a real conviction
to receive. When you see a humped-over person crawling
through the crowd, know that that person really wants
help. That kind of desire is what it takes to change your
life. Jesus is the answer. It doesn't matter what the problem is, He is the answer.

What time I am afraid, I will trust in thee.

Psalm 56:3

Fear is as lethal to us as paralysis of the brain. It makes our thoughts become arthritic and our memory sluggish. It is the kind of feeling that can make a graceful person stumble up the stairs in a crowd. You know what I mean—the thing that makes the articulate stutter and the rhythmic become spastic. Like an oversized growth, fear soon becomes impossible to camouflage. Telltale signs like trembling knees or quivering lips betray fear even in the most disciplined person.

Fear traps time and holds it hostage in a prison of icy anxiety. Eventually, though, like the thawing of icicles on a roof, a heart can gradually melt into a steady and less pronounced beat.

I confess that maturity has chased away many of the ghosts and goblins of my youthful closet of fear. Nevertheless, there are still those occasional moments when reason gives way to the fanciful imagination of the fearful little boy in me, who peeks his head out of my now fully developed frame like a turtle sticks his head out of its shell with caution and precision.

And besought Him that they might only touch the hem of His garment: and as many as touched were made perfectly whole.

Matthew 14:36

———

There's a place in God where the Lord will touch you and provide intimacy in your life when you're not getting it from other places. You must be open to His touch. If you can't receive from Him, you may find yourself like the woman at the well, who sought physical gratification (see John 4:18). If you seek only the physical when you really need intimacy, what you end up getting is simply sex. Sex is a poor substitute for intimacy. It's nice with intimacy, but when it is substituted for intimacy, it's frustrating.

Likewise, we are snared by the words in our own mouth. The enemy would love to destroy you with your own words. He will use your strength against you. Many of you have beat yourself down with the power of your own words. The enemy worked you against yourself until you saw yourself as crippled. Reverse his plan. If you had enough force to bend yourself, you've got enough force to straighten yourself back up again.

*And the Gentiles shall see thy righteousness, and
all kings thy glory: and thou shalt be called by a
new name, which the mouth of the Lord shall name.*

Isaiah 62:2

Jacob was his mother's darling. He was what we would
call a "momma's boy."

Jacob, whose name meant "supplanter" or "trickster,"
literally "con man," was left alone with God. God cannot accomplish anything with us until we are left alone
with Him. There, in the isolation of our internal strife,
God begins the process of transforming disgrace into
grace. It only took a midnight rendezvous and an
encounter with a God he couldn't "out slick" to bring
Jacob's leg to a limp and his fist to a hand clasped in
prayer. "I won't let You go till You bless me," he cries.
God then tells him what he really needs to know. He
tells Jacob that he is not who he thinks he is. In fact, he
is really Israel, a prince. (See Genesis 32:24-30.)

My friend, when we, like Jacob, seek to know God, He
will inevitably show us our real identity. My friend, if no
one else knows who you are, God knows.

The Lord is my light and my salvation; whom shall I fear? The Lord is the strength of my life; of whom shall I be afraid? When the wicked, even mine enemies and my foes, came upon me to eat up my flesh, they stumbles and fell....

Psalm 27:1-3

Sometimes pain can become too familiar. Ungodly relationships often become familiar. Change doesn't come easily. Habits and patterns are hard to break. Sometimes we maintain relationships because we fear change. However, when we see our value the way Jesus sees us, we muster the courage to break away.

He will defend you before your critics. Now is the time for you to focus on receiving the miraculous and getting the water that you could not get before. He is loosing you to water. You haven't been drinking for 18 years, but now you can get a drink. With Jesus, you can do it.

Some of you have been a pack horse for many years. People have dumped on you. You've never been allowed to develop without stress and weights, not just because of the circumstances, but because of how deeply things affect you. Our God, however, is a liberator.

My little children, of whom I travail in birth again until Christ be formed in you.

Galatians 4:19

God understands the hidden part within us. In spite of our growth, income, education, or notoriety, He still speaks to the childhood issues of the aging heart. This is the ministry that only a Father can give.

The Lord looks beyond our facade and sees the trembling places in our lives. He knows our innermost needs. No matter how spiritually mature we try to appear, He is still aware that lurking in the shadows is a discarded desire we just prayed off last night—the lingering evidence of some temper or temptation that only the Father can see hiding within His supposedly "all grown-up" little child.

It is He alone who can see the very worst in us, yet still think the very best of us. It is the unfailing love of a Father whose son should have been old enough to receive his inheritance without acting like a child, without wandering off into failure. Nevertheless, the Father's love throws a party for the prodigal and prepares a feast for the foolish. Comprehend with childhood faith the love of the Father!

Now the Lord had said unto Abram, Get thee out of thy country, and from thy kindred, and from thy father's house, unto a land that I will show thee: and I will make of thee a great nation, and I will bless thee, and make thy name great; and thou shalt be a blessing....

Genesis 12:1-3

You must reach the point where it is the Lord whom you desire. Singleness of heart will bring about deliverance. Perhaps you have spent all your time and effort trying to prove yourself to someone who is gone. Maybe an old lover left you with scars. The person may be dead and buried, but you are still trying to win his approval.

In this case, you are dedicated to worthless tasks. You are committed to things, unattainable goals, that will not satisfy. Christ must be your ambition. For some things you don't have time to recover gradually. The moment you get the truth, you are loosed.

Once you realize that you have been unleashed, you will feel a sudden change. When you come to Jesus, He will motivate you. You need to blossom and come forth.

Set your affection on things above, not on things on the earth. For ye are dead, and your life is hid with Christ in God.

Colossians 3:2-3

The new birth is not a change on your birth certificate; it is a change in your heart. In this sense we have a name change as it pertains to our character.

A name is important. It tells something about your origin or your destiny. You don't want just anyone to name you. Many of God's people are walking under the stigma of their old nature's name. That wretched feeling associated with what others called you or thought about you can limit you as you reach for greatness. However, it is not what others think that matters. You want to be sure, even if you are left alone and no one knows but you, to know who the Father says you are. Knowing your new name is for your own edification. When the enemy gets out his list and starts naming your past, tell him, "Haven't you heard? The person you knew died! I am not who he was and I am certainly not what he did!"

*We give thanks to God always for you all, making
mention of you in our prayers; remembering without ceasing your work of faith, and labor of love,
and patience of hope in our Lord Jesus Christ, in
the sight of God and our Father.*

1 Thessalonians 1:2-3

Faith is an equal opportunity business. There is no dis-
crimination in it. Faith will work for you. When you
approach God, don't worry about the fact that you are a
woman. Never become discouraged on that basis when it
comes to seeking Him. You will only get as much from
God as you can believe Him for.

He wants you to believe Him. He is trying to teach you
so when the time for a real miracle does come, you'll
have some faith to draw from. God wants you to understand that if you can believe Him, you can go from
defeat to victory and from poverty to prosperity!

Faith is more than a fact—faith is an action. When you
finally understand that you are loose, you will start
behaving as if you were set free. You are whole; you are
loose. You can go anywhere.

He shall feed His flock like a shepherd: He shall gather the lambs with His arm, and carry them in His bosom, and shall gently lead those that are with young.

Isaiah 40:11

When the disciples asked Jesus to teach them to pray, the first thing He taught them was to acknowledge the fatherhood of God. When we say "Our Father," we acknowledge His fatherhood and declare our sonship. We need to know not only who our father is, but how he feels about us.

I can still remember what it was like to fall asleep watching television and have my father carry me up the stairs to bed. I never felt as safe and protected as I did in the arms of my father—that is, until he died and I was forced to seek refuge in the arms of my Heavenly Father.

What a relief to learn that God can carry the load even better than my natural father could, and that He will never leave me nor forsake me! Perhaps this inspired the hymnist to pen, "What a fellowship, what a joy divine. Leaning on the everlasting arms" ("Leaning On the Everlasting Arms," Elisha A. Hoffman, 1887).

Now faith is the substance of things hoped for, the evidence of things not seen. For by it the elders obtained a good report.

Hebrews 11:1-2

Hebrews chapter 11 is a faith "hall of fame." It lists great people of God who believed Him and accomplished great exploits.

There are two contrasting women mentioned in the faith "hall of fame." Sarah, Abraham's wife, is listed. Rahab, the Jericho prostitute, is listed as well. A married woman and a whore made it to the hall of fame. A godly woman and a whore made it into the book. I understand why Sarah was included, but how in the world did this prostitute get to be honored? She was listed because God does not honor morality. He honors faith. That was the one thing they had in common; nothing else.

Rahab didn't have a husband. She had the whole city. Sarah stayed in the tent and knit socks. There was no similarity in their lifestyles, just in their faith. God saw something in Sarah that He also saw in Rahab. Do not accept the excuse that because you have lived like a Rahab you can't have the faith experience.

Even though you have ten thousand guardians in Christ, you do not have many fathers, for in Christ Jesus I became your father through the gospel.

1 Corinthians 4:15 NIV

We must know the difference between guardians and fathers. Paul said that he became their father through the Gospel. What does this mean?

Boys are nurtured by their mothers, but they receive their identity and definition of masculinity from their fathers! Thank God for the mothers in the Church—but where are our fathers? We have raised a generation of young men who couldn't find their natural fathers and now they struggle with their spiritual fathers.

It is difficult to develop healthy spiritual authority in the heart of a man who hasn't seen healthy male relationships. Such men tend to be overly sensitive or rebellious, quickly associating authority with abuse as that may be their only past experience. To you men, whether younger or older, who still wrestle with these issues, allow the hand of your Heavenly Father to heal the abuse and neglect of your earthly fathers. God is so wise that He will give you a spiritual father to fill the voids in your life. Trust Him!

Looking unto Jesus the author and finisher of our faith....

Hebrews 12:2a

God wants you to believe Him. Make a decision and stand on it. Rahab decided to take a stand on the side of God's people. She hid the spies. She made the decision based on her faith. She took action. Faith is a fact and faith is an action. She took action because she believed God would deliver her when Jericho fell to the Israelites.

God wants your faith to be developed. Faith is an equal opportunity business. No matter how many mistakes you have made, it is still faith that God honors. You may have been like Rahab, but if you can believe God, He will save your house. You know, He didn't save only her; He saved her entire household. All the other homes in Jericho were destroyed.

You would have thought He would have saved some nice little lady's house. Perhaps He would have saved some cottage housing an old woman, or a little widow's house, with petunias growing on the sidewalk. No, God saved the whore's house. Was it because He wanted it? No, He wanted the faith. That is what moves God.

...and to know the love of Christ, which passeth knowledge, that ye might be filled with all the fullness of God.

Ephesians 3:19

The Bible declares that we should have a strong degree of reverence for God. "Reverence" means to respect or revere; "fear" has the connotation of terror and intimidation. That kind of fear is not a healthy attitude for a child of God to have about his Heavenly Father. The term rendered "fear" in Job 28:28 could be better translated as "respect."

Fear will drive man away from God like it drove Adam to hide in the bushes at the sound of the voice of his only Deliverer. Adam said, *"I heard Thy voice in the garden, and I was afraid..."* (Gen. 3:10). That is not the reaction a loving father wants from his children. I don't want my children to scatter and hide when I approach! I may not always agree with what they have done, but I will always love who they are. He may not approve of your conduct, but He still loves you! In fact, when you come to understand this fact, it will help you improve your conduct.

Now the just shall live by faith: but if any man draw back, my soul shall have no pleasure in him.
Hebrews 10:38

If you believe that your background will keep you from moving forward with God, then you don't understand the value of faith. The thing God is asking from you is faith. Some may live good, clean, separated lives.

If you want to grasp the things of God, you will not be able to purely because of your lifestyle, but because of your conviction. God gave healing to some folks who weren't even saved. They were sinners. Perhaps some of them never did get saved, but they got healed because they believed Him.

And Joshua saved Rahab the harlot alive, and her father's household, and all that she had; and she dwelleth in Israel even unto this day; because she hid the messengers, which Joshua sent to spy out Jericho.
Joshua 6:25

There was something in Rahab's house that God called valuable. Faith was there. The thing that moves God is faith. If you believe Him, He will move in your life according to your faith and not to your experience.

And they journeyed from Bethel; and there was but a little way to come to Ephraph: and Rachel travailed, and she had hard labor.... And it came to pass, as her soul was departing, (for she died) that she called his name Benoni: but his father called him Benjamin.

Genesis 35:16-18

Jacob, now Israel, has come to a point of resting in his God-given identity. Israel has seasoned and matured. He has produced many strong sons. One son is yet inside the love of his life, Rachel, who is in the final stages of pregnancy. Before they could reach their destination, Rachel births a son. Just before she dies, Rachel looks at her baby and names him Benoni, which means "son of my sorrow."

Jacob's eyes turn deeply within. Perhaps he remembers what a wrong name can do to a child. He speaks with the wisdom that is born out of personal experience. "He shall not be called Benoni, son of my sorrow. He shall be called Benjamin, son of my right hand. He is my strength, not my sorrow!" he declares. Guess whose name prevailed, Benjamin; you are who your father says you are.

Wherefore come out from among them, and be ye separate, saith the Lord, and touch not the unclean thing; and I will receive you, and will be a Father unto you, and ye shall be My sons and daughters, saith the Lord Almighty.

2 Corinthians 6:17.

There were a group of sisters in the Old Testament who proved that God was interested in what happens to women.

There were no men left in the family. Their father had wealth, but he had no sons. Prior to this time, women were not allowed to own property or to have an inheritance except through their husbands. Only men could own property.

They appealed, *"Why should the name of our father be done away from among his family, because he hath no son? Give unto us therefore a possession among the brethren of our father"* (Num. 27:4).

They appealed to Moses for help. They stated their case and looked to him as God's authority. They would have been poor and homeless, receiving only leftovers from others. However, these women were daughters of Abraham. If you want the enemy to release you, remind him whose daughter you are.

*Wherefore God also hath highly exalted Him, and
given Him a name which is above every name that
at the name of Jesus every knee should bow; of
things in heaven, and things in earth, and things
under the earth.*

Philippians 2:9,10

In the name of Jesus you must break the spell of every
name that would attach itself to you. If your Heavenly
Father didn't give you that name, then it isn't right. You
are who He says you are. Rest in the identity that He
places upon you. No one knew any better than
Jacob/Israel the power of a name change! Remember, it
was in his Father's presence that he discovered he was
not a trickster, but a prince! When you believe on the
covenant name of Jesus, you break the strength of every
other name that would attach itself to your identity. In
the early Church, entire cities were delivered from
satanic attack in that name. Even today, drug addicts, les-
bians, pimps, and every other name is subject to the
name of the Lord. His name is strong enough to break
the bondage of any other name that would attach itself to
your life.

And...the scribes and Pharisees...said...How is it that he eateth and drinketh with publicans and sinners?

Mark 2:16

Then came the daughters of Zelophehad, who asked for the inheritance from their father. There were no sons to claim the inheritance. No one would have listened to them if they had not initiated a meeting to plead their case. Perhaps you who have struggled need to call a meeting. Get in touch with people in power and demand what you want, or you will not get it. Speak for yourself. They could not understand why they were being discriminated against because of their gender.

It was time to teach God's people that women have value. Abraham's daughters have worth. They didn't wait for a man to defend them; they took action in faith. God saw faith in those women.

Moses didn't know what to do, so he asked God. The women were vindicated. If they had failed, surely they would have been scorned by all the good people of Israel who would have never challenged Moses in such a way. Instead they received the wealth of their father. God is no respecter of persons. Faith is based on equal opportunity.

*And God shall wipe away all tears from their eyes;
and there shall be no more death, neither sorrow, nor
crying, neither shall there be any more pain: for the
former things are passed away. And He that sat
upon the throne said, Behold, I make all things new.*

Revelation 21:4-5

If you are wrestling with the curse and stigma of public
opinion, you don't have to stay the way you are. The
Potter wants to put you back together again. God is a
God of second chances.

This good news is that God changes names. Throughout
the Scriptures He took men like Abram, the exalted
father, and transformed his image and character into
Abraham, the father of many nations. There is a place in
your walk with God—a place of discipleship—whereby
God radically changes your character. With that change
He can erase the stigma of your past and give you a
fresh name in your community—but most importantly,
in your heart. Get on your knees and wrestle with Him
in prayer until you can arise knowing what He knows.
Rise up from prayer knowing who you really are in the
Spirit and in the Kingdom.

The eyes of your understanding being enlightened;
that ye may know what is the hope of His calling,
and what the riches of the glory of His inheritance
in the saints.

Ephesians 1:18

You want the inheritance of your father to pass on to you. Why should you sit there and be in need when your Father has left you everything? Your Father is rich, and He left everything to you. However, you will not get your inheritance until you ask for it. Demand what your father left you. That degree, that promotion, that financial breakthrough has your name on it.

The power to get wealth is in your tongue. You shall have whatever you say. If you keep sitting around murmuring, groaning, and complaining, you use your tongue against yourself. Open your mouth and speak something good about yourself. Begin to speak deliverance and power. You are not defeated. You are Abraham's daughter.

When you start speaking correctly, God will give you what you say. You say you want it. God willed you something. Your Father left you an inheritance. If God would bless the sons of Abraham, surely He would bless the daughters of Abraham.

*I am come in My Father's name, and ye receive Me
not: if another shall come in his own name, him ye
will receive.*

John 5:43

The Word of the Lord often stands alone. It has no
attorney and it needs no witness. It can stand on its
own merit. Whatever He says, you are! If you are to fight
the challenge of this age, then shake the enemy's names
and insults off your shoulder. Look the enemy in the eye
without guilt or timidity and declare:

"I have not come clothed in the vesture of my past. Nor
will I use the opinions of this world for my defense. No,
I am far wiser through the things I have suffered. Therefore I have come in my Father's name. He has anointed
my head, counseled my fears, and taught me who I am. I
am covered by His anointing, comforted by His presence, and kept by His auspicious grace. Today, as never
before, I stand in the identity He has given me and
renounce every memory of who I was yesterday. I was
called for such a time as this, and I have come in my
Father's name!"

For as many of you as have been baptized into Christ have put on Christ. There is neither Jew nor Greek, there is neither bond nor free, there is neither male nor female: for ye are all one in Christ Jesus.

Galatians 3:27-28

"For ye are all the children of God by faith in Christ Jesus" (Gal. 3:26). Women are just as much children of God as men are. Everything that God will do for a man, He will do for a woman. You are not disadvantaged. You can get an inheritance like any man. Generally men don't cry about being single—they simply get on with life and stay busy. There is no reason a woman can't be complete in God without a husband.

If you choose to get married, you should get married for the right reasons. You need someone who has some shoulders and backbone. You need to marry someone who will hold you, help you, strengthen you, build you up, and be with you when the storms of life are raging. If you want a cute man, buy a photograph. If you want some help, marry a godly man.

> But ye are a chosen generation, a royal priesthood, an holy nation, a peculiar people; that ye should show forth the praises of Him who hath called you out of darkness into His marvelous light: which in time past were not a people, but are now the people of God: which had not obtained mercy, but now have obtained mercy.
>
> 1 Peter 2:9-10

The infirm woman in Luke 13 was bowed over until Jesus touched her. Once He touched her, she stood up. You have put on Christ. There is no reason to be bent over after His touch. You can walk with respect even when you have past failures. It's not what people say about you that makes you different. It is what you say about yourself, and what your God has said about you that really matters.

Just because someone calls you a tramp doesn't mean you have to act like one. You can't help where you've been, but you can help where you're going. And God is not concerned about race. Real spiritual advantage does not come from the color of your skin. The content of your heart brings deliverance and help from God.

Therefore being justified by faith, we have peace with God through our Lord Jesus Christ: by whom also we have access by faith into this grace wherein we stand, and rejoice in hope of the glory of God.

Romans 5:1-2

Some of us have particular problems based on where we came from. We've got to deal with it. God says there is neither Greek nor Jew. There is no such thing as a Black church. There is no such thing as a White church. It's only one Church, purchased by the blood of the Lamb. We are all one in Christ Jesus.

You may have been born with a silver spoon in your mouth too, but it doesn't make any difference. In the Kingdom of God, social status doesn't mean anything. Faith is the only thing in this world where there is true equal opportunity. Everyone can come to Jesus.

"There is neither male nor female" (Gal. 3:28). God doesn't look at your gender. He looks at your heart. He doesn't look at morality and good works. He looks at the faith that lives within. God is looking in your heart. All people are one in Christ Jesus.

Lo, children are an heritage of the Lord: and the fruit of the womb is his reward. As arrows are in the hand of a mighty man; so are children of the youth. Happy is the man that hath his quiver full of them....

Psalm 127:3-5

The psalmist David wrote a brief note that speaks to the heart of men about their attitude toward their offspring. David is the man who prayed feverishly for mercy as his child squirmed in the icy hands of death. If anybody knows the value of children, it is those who just left theirs in the ground. "As arrows are in the hand of a mighty man; so are children of the youth," says King David whose arrow they lowered in the ground.

Why did he compare children to arrows? Maybe it was for their potential to be propelled into the future. Maybe he was trying to tell us that children go where we, their parents, aim them. Parents, must be responsible to place them in the kind of bow that will accelerate their success and emotional well-being? How happy I am to have a quiver full of arrows.

Be careful in your life and in your teaching. If you continue to live and teach rightly, you will save both yourself and those who listen to you.

1 Timothy 4:16 NCV

Once a young lady, who had been attending my church, came to me in tears. She had been brutally raped by several young men. She told me that the hospital gave her what they call a morning-after pill to stop the possibility of her being pregnant as a result of this tragedy. I later learned that this pill is designed to kill any possibility of pregnancy after rape. I scarcely knew how to counsel her.

I mentioned her because I wish there was a spiritual morning-after pill we could get to kill the unwanted spiritual embryos left behind from our previous associations with dead things. Since we have succeeded in destroying our relationships with the past, let's deal with all those side effects that resulted from our previous infidelities. There can be progeny born in us from our relationships with the past; they must be sought out and destroyed. These offsprings of another time when we were less spiritually mature cannot be allowed to exist in us.

Let them melt away as waters which run continually: when he bendeth his bow to show his arrows....

Psalm 58:7

It is for the arrows of this generation that we must pray—they who are being aimed at the streets and drugs and perversion. Not all of them, but some of them have been broken in the quiver!

If someone must be hurt, if it ever becomes necessary to bear pains or withstand trials, let it be adults and not children. I can accept the fate before me. I was my father's arrow and my mother's heart. My father is dead, but his arrows are yet soaring in the wind. You will never know him; he is gone. However, my brother, my sister, and I are scientific proof that he was, and through us, continues to be. I am an arrow shot. I have had the greatest riches known to man. I have had an opportunity to test the limits of my destiny. Whether preferred or rejected, let the record show: I am here. Oh, God, let me hit my target! But if I miss and plummet to the ground, then at least I can say, "I have been shot!"

For His anger endureth but a moment; in His favor is life: weeping may endure for a night, but joy cometh in the morning

Psalm 30:5

———

David said that if we could hold out, joy comes in the morning. The bad news is, everybody has a bad night at one time or another. The good news is there will be a morning after. Allow the joy of the morning light to push away any unwanted partners, curses, or fears that stop you from achieving your goal.

So let the hungry mouth of failure's offspring meet the dry breast of a Christian who has determined to overcome the past. In order for these embryos of destruction to survive, they must be fed. They feed on the fears and insecurities of people who haven't declared their liberty.

Once you realize that you are the source from which it draws its milk, you regain control. Feed what you want to live and starve what you want to die! Why not think positively until every negative thing that is a result of dead issues turns blue and releases its grip on your home and your destiny? It's your mind. You've got the power.

The Spirit of God has made me, and the breath of the Almighty gives me life.

Job 33:4 NKJV

In the ministry, there is a different prerequisite for effectiveness than what the textbooks alone can provide. It is not a medicine compiled by a pharmacist that is needed for the patients lying on the tables of my heart. We don't need medicine; we need miracles. Many have more faith in a textbook written by a person whose eyes may be clouded by their own secrets, than to rely upon the Word of a God who knows the end from the beginning.

If there is something minor wrong with my car, like a radiator hose needing replaced or a tire changed, I can take it almost anywhere. But if I suspect there is trouble with it, I always take it to the dealer. The manufacturer knows his product better than the average mechanic. So like the dealership, ministers may work with, but need not be intimidated by, the sciences of the mind! God is not practicing. He is accomplished. I want to share God-given, biblical answers to troubling questions as we deal with the highly sensitive areas counseling.

For as he thinketh in his heart, so he is.

Proverbs 23:7a

If there be any virtue, and if there be any praise, think on these things.

Philippians 4:8

In this verse, Paul teaches thought modification. He taught that if we exercise the discipline of thought modification, we can produce internal or intrinsic excellence. The phrase, *"if there be any virtue,"* suggests that if there is to be any intrinsic excellence, we must modify our thoughts to think on the things he mentioned first.

The term virtue refers to intrinsic excellence. That means people who are filled with excellence achieve that excellence by the thoughts they have about themselves and about the world around them. Thoughts are powerful. They feed the seeds of greatness that are in the womb of our minds. They also can nurse the negative insecurities that limit us and exempt us from greatness. There is a virtue that comes from tranquil, peaceful thoughts that build positive character in the heart. As a rule, people who are cynical and vicious tend to be unsuccessful. If they are successful, they don't really feel their success because their cynicism robs from them the sweet taste of reward.

He hath made His wonderful works to be remembered: the Lord is gracious and full of compassion.

Psalm 111:4

I earnestly believe that where there is no compassion, there can be no lasting change. As long as Christian leadership secretly jeers and sneers at the perversion that comes into the Church, there will be no healing. The enemy robs us of our healing power by robbing us of our concern.

Compassion is the mother of miracles! When the storm had troubled the waters and Peter thought he would die, he didn't challenge Christ's power; he challenged His compassion. He went into the back side of the ship and said, *"Carest Thou not that we perish?"* (Mark 4:38) He understood that if there is no real compassion, then there can be no miracle.

Until we, as priests, are touched with the feelings of our parishioners' illnesses rather than just turned off by their symptoms, they will not be healed. To every husband who wants to see his wife healed, to every mother who has a little girl with a woman's problem: The power to heal is in the power to care. Rise and be healed in the name of Jesus.

How precious also are Thy thoughts unto me, O God! How great is the sum of them!

Psalm 139:17

Thoughts are powerful. They feed the seeds of greatness that are in the womb of our minds. They also can nurse the negative insecurities that limit us and exempt us from greatness. There is a virtue that comes from peaceful thoughts that build positive character in the heart. As a rule, people who are cynical and vicious tend to be unsuccessful. If they are successful, they don't really feel their success because their cynicism robs from them the sweet taste of reward.

Thoughts are secrets hidden behind quick smiles and professional veneers. They are a private world that others cannot invade. None of us would be comfortable at having all our thoughts played aloud for the whole world to hear. Yet our thoughts can accurately forecast approaching success or failure. No one can hear God think, but we can feel the effects of His thoughts toward us. Like sprouts emerging from enriched soil, our words and eventually our actions push through the fertilized fields of our innermost thoughts. Like our Creator we deeply affect others by our thoughts toward them.

The Lord upholdeth all that fall, and raiseth up all those that be bowed down.

Psalm 145:14

And Jesus, moved with compassion, put for His hand, and touched him, and saith unto him, I will; be thou clean.

Mark 1:41

Preceding miracle after miracle, compassion provoked power. We can no longer ostracize the victim and let the assailant escape! Every time you see some insecure, vulnerable, intimidated adult who has unnatural fear in her eyes, low self-esteem or an apologetic posture, she is saying, "Carest thou not that I perish?" Every time you see a bra-less woman in men's jeans, choosing to act like a man rather than to sleep with one; every time you see a handsome young man who could have been someone's father, walking like someone's mother—you may be looking child abuse in the face.

If you think it's ugly, you're right. If you think it's wrong, you're right again. If you think it can't be healed, you're dead wrong! If you look closely into these eyes I've so feebly tried to describe, you will sense that something in this person is weak, hurt, maimed, or disturbed, but fixable.

But by the grace of God I am what I am....
1 Corinthians 15:10a

———

Some years ago I was birthing my ministry in terms of evangelism.... It was not at all uncommon for me to drive for hours into some rural, secluded "backwoods" area to minister to a handful of people who were often financially, and in some cases mentally, deprived!

Once, I encountered some children who were either physically or mentally abnormal. These abnormalities ranged in severity from slurred speech to missing fingers and dwarfed limbs.

Suddenly I began to understand that these children were the result of inordinate affections and incestuous relationships.... This plight could have been avoided. So are the children of the mind: the crippled need we sometimes have to receive accolades; the angry tears that flood because we are left holding the offspring of yesterday's mistakes in our arms. We wonder what we could have been if one thing or another had not happened.

God teaches men character in the most deplorable of classrooms. I thought I was traveling to minister to the people, but God was taking me through a series of hurdles in order to strengthen my legs for the sprints ahead.

He healeth the broken in heart, and bindeth up their wounds.

Psalm 147:3

Splintered, broken arrows come in all colors and forms. Some are black, some white; some are rich, some poor. One thing about pain, though: It isn't prejudiced. To God be the glory. He is a magnificent Healer!

Each person who has been through these adversities has her own story. Some have been blessed by not having to experience any such circumstance. Let the strong bear the infirmities of the weak. God can greatly use you to restore wholeness to others who walk in varying degrees of brokenness. To those who have fallen prey to satan's snares, we teach righteousness while still loving the unrighteous. Most of us have had some degree of damage. The fact that we have persevered is a testimony.

Anything hurt, is unhappy. We cannot get a wounded lion to jump through hoops! Hurting children and hurting adults can carry the unpleasant aroma of bitterness.

Even if you were exposed to grown-up situations when you were a child, God can reverse what you've been through. He'll let the grown-up person experience the joy of being a child in the presence of God!

> *(For the weapons of our warfare are not carnal, but*
> *mighty through God to the pulling down of strong*
> *holds;) casting down imaginations, and every high*
> *thing that exalteth itself against the knowledge of*
> *God, and bringing into captivity every though to*
> *the obedience of Christ.*
>
> 2 Corinthians 10:4-5

God has given you power over the enemy! He has given you the power to abort the seeds of failure. Pull down those things that have taken a strong hold in your life. If you don't pull them down, they will refuse to relinquish their grip. It will take an act of your will and God's power to stop the spiritual unborn from manifesting in your life. God will not do it without you—but He will do it through you….

The greatest freedom you have is the freedom to change your mind. Repentance is when the mind decides to overthrow the government that controlled it in the past. As long as these other things reign in your life, they are sitting on the throne. If they are on the throne, then Christ is on the Cross. Put Christ on the throne and your past on the Cross.

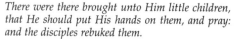

There were there brought unto Him little children,
that He should put His hands on them, and pray:
and the disciples rebuked them.

Matthew 19:13

It is interesting to me that just before this took place the
Lord was ministering on the subject of divorce and
adultery. When He brought up that subject, someone
brought the children to Him so He could touch them.

Who were these nameless persons who had the insight
and the wisdom to bring the children to the Master?
They brought the children to Him that He might touch
them. What a strange interruption to a discourse on adultery and divorce. Here are these little children dragging
dirty blankets and blank gazes into the presence of a God
who is dealing with grown-up problems. He takes time
from His busy schedule not so much to counsel them,
but just to touch them. That's all it takes. Don't forget to
touch their little lives with a word of hope and a smile of
encouragement. It may be the only one some will
receive. You are the builders of our future. Be careful, for
you may be building a house that we will have to live in!

This people have I formed for Myself; they shall show forth My praise.

Isaiah 43:21

Above all titles and professions, every Christian is called to be a worshiper. We are a royal priesthood that might have become extinct had the mercy of the Lord not arrested the horrors of the enemy. Calloused hands are raised in praise—hands that tell a story of struggle, whether spiritual or natural…. Who could better thank the Lord than the oppressed who were delivered by the might of a loving God whose love is tempered with the necessary ability to provoke change.

The intensity of our praise is born out of the ever-freshness of our memories, not so much of our past, but of His mercies toward us.

Woe be to the priest who tries to have a fresh worship experience while constantly reliving the dead issues of the past. In that case the memories become an obstacle around your neck. What would it matter for all the voices in the earth to commend you for your contributions, if God disagreed? Lift up your head and be blessed in the presence of the Lord. Nothing is nearly as important as ministering to the Lord.

And they brought young children to Him, that He should touch them: and His disciples rebuked those that brought them. But when Jesus saw it, He was much displeased, and said unto them, Suffer the little children to come unto Me, and forbid them not: for of such is the kingdom of God…and he took them up in his arms, put his hands upon them, and blessed them.

Mark 10:13-16

What is wrong with these disciples that they became angry at some nameless person who aimed these little arrows at the only answer they might ever have gotten to see? Who told them they were too busy to heal their own children? The time has come for us to suffer the suffering to come. They brought the "ouch" to the Band-Aid, and He stopped His message for His mission. They came to get a touch, but He always gives us more than we expected. He blessed them with His compassionate heart!

When Jesus blessed the children, He challenged the adults to become as children. We need to allow ourselves the kind of relationship with God that we may have missed as a child. God provides arms that allow grown children to climb up like children and be nurtured through the tragedies of early days.

And such were some of you: but ye are washed, but ye are sanctified, but ye are justified in the name of the Lord Jesus, and by the Spirit of our God.

1 Corinthians 6:11

In the early Church, the disciples experienced awesome displays of power that we don't seem to experience to the same degree. Few of us are walking in enough light to cast the kind of shadow that causes others to be healed.... What is wrong? We have become a nation of priests who spend too much time touching the dead and not enough washing our hearts with pure water!

Give your heart a bath. Submerge it deeply into the purity of God's Word and scrub away the remaining debris of deathly ills and concerns. These may be stopping you from participating in the greatest move of God that this generation will ever see! A clouded heart cannot move into the realm of faith. It takes clarity to flow in divine authority. Satan knows that pureness of heart is necessary to see God. These distresses and stresses are spiritual cholesterol! They will stop the heart from being able to see God.

Because thou shalt forget thy misery, and remember it as waters that pass away.

Job 11:16

It is inconceivable to the injured that the injury can be forgotten. To forget isn't to develop amnesia. It is to reach a place where the misery is pulled from the memory as a stinger pulled out of an insect bite. Once the stinger is gone, healing is inevitable. This passage says that the memory is as "waters that pass away." Stand in a stream with waters around your ankles. The waters that pass by you at that moment, you will never see again. So it is with the misery that has challenged your life: Let it go, let it pass away. The brilliance of morning is in sharp contrast to the darkness of night; simply stated, it was night, but now it is day. David understood the aftereffects of traumatic deliverance when he said, *"Weeping may endure for a night, but joy cometh in the morning"* (Ps. 30:5b).

It is when we become secure in our relationship with God that we begin to allow the past to fall from us as a garment. We remember it, but choose not to wear it!

And though after my skin worms destroy this body,
yet in my flesh shall I see God: whom I shall see for
myself, and mine eyes shall behold, and not
another; though my reins be consumed within me.

Job 19:26-27

If the worshiper, has so many unresolved issues on his heart, how can he see God?

This Scripture clearly draws a line of prerequisites necessary to see God in His fullest sense. God's invisibility doesn't refer to an inability to be seen as much as it does to your inability to behold Him. To the blind all things are invisible. How can I see this God who cannot be detected in my vision's periphery? Jesus taught that a pure heart could see God. No wonder David cried out, *"Create in me a clean heart..."* (Ps. 51:10).

The term used in Matthew 5:8 for pure comes from the Greek word *katharos*, which means "to clean out," much like a laxative. Don't carry around what God wants discarded. Get rid of *"every weight, and the sin which doth so easily beset us"* (Heb. 12:1)! What God wants to unveil to you is worth the cleaning up to see.

*None of you shall approach to any that is near of kin
to him, to uncover their nakedness: I am the Lord.*

Leviticus 18:6

Eve was meant to be covered and originally Adam was
her covering, to nurture and protect her. If someone
"uncovered" you, there is a feeling of being violated.
Even when these feelings are suppressed, and they often
are, they are still powerful. Sexual abuse violates the
covering of the family and the responsible persons whom
we looked to for guidance. This stripping away of right
relation leaves us exposed to the infinite reality of corrupt, lustful imaginations. Like fruit peeled too soon, it
is damaging to uncover what God had wanted to remain
protected! Who among us can repeel a banana once it
has been peeled? The Bible says, *"With men it is impossible, but not with God: for with God all things are possible"* (Mark 10:27).

Do you realize that one of the things the blood of Jesus
Christ does is cover us? Like Noah's sons who covered
their father's nakedness, the blood of Jesus will cover the
uncovered. He will not allow you to spend the rest of
your life exposed.

*If any man's work shall be burned, he shall suffer
loss: but he himself shall be saved; yet so as by fire.*
1 Corinthians 3:15

If you gaze deep into a fire you will notice that the
sparks leave the burning log as hot as the fire itself.
They swirl into the chimney into the dark chambers
above. But these flickering lights are soon extinguished
by being separated from their source. How many Christians explode into the brilliancy of worship and praise,
but are soon dark and cold, losing their first fire? Stay in
the fire, my friend, where the other embers can share
their heat with you and keep you ablaze! It is the fire of
God that will assist you in burning up the offspring, the
oddities, and the obstacles of yesteryear.

Perhaps that is what happened in the fiery furnace with
the Hebrew boys. The fire was on assignment. It could
burn only what was an obstacle hindering those who
refused to worship idols from worshiping God. Some
people He saves from the fire; praise God for them. But
all too often God saves most of us by the fire!

Because God wanted to make the unchanging
nature of His purpose very clear to the heirs of
what was promised, He confirmed it with an oath.
God did this so that, by two unchangeable things
in which it is impossible for God to lie, we who
have fled to take hold of the hope offered to us may
be greatly encouraged.

Hebrews 6:17-18 NIV

Reach out and embrace the fact that God has been watching over you all of your life. My sister, He covers you and He blesses you! Rejoice in Him in spite of the broken places. God's grace is sufficient for your needs and your scars. He will anoint you with oil. May it bathe, heal, and strengthen you as never before.

There will be a time in your life when God nurtures you through crisis situations. You may not even realize how many times God has intervened to relieve the tensions and stresses of day-to-day living. Every now and then He does us a favor—something we didn't earn or can't even explain. He knows when the load is overwhelming. Many times He moves (it seems to us) just in the nick of time.

Whom God hath set forth to be a propitiation through faith in His blood, to declare His righteousness for the remission of sins that are past, through the forbearance of God.

Romans 3:25

God wants to bring you to a place of rest, where there is no pacing the floor, no glaring at those with whom you are involved, through frightened eyes.

There is no torment like inner torment. How can you run from yourself? No matter what you achieve in life, if the old ghosts are not laid to rest, you will not have any real sense of peace and inner joy. God says, "None shall make thee afraid." A *"perfect love casts out fear"!* (See 1 John 4:18.) It is a miserable feeling to spend your life in fear. Fear can manifest itself in jealousy, depression, and many other distresses. As you allow the past to pass over you as waters moving in the sea, you will begin to live and rest in a new assurance. Take authority over every flashback and every dream that keeps you linked to the past. The peace of God will do a new thing in your life.

And they shall be Mine, saith the Lord of hosts, in that day when I make up My jewels; and I will spare them, as a man spareth his own son that serveth him.

Malachi 3:17

I was raised in the rich, robust Appalachian mountains of West Virginia which was the backyard for many Indians in days gone by. During my childhood, occasionally either my classmates or myself would find old Indian memorabilia in the rocks and creek beds. The most common thing to find would be discarded arrowheads. Perhaps an Indian brave had thrown away the arrow, assuming he had gotten out of it all the possible use he could. Though worthless to him, it was priceless to us as we retrieved it from its hiding place and saved it. I believe that God gathers discarded children who, like arrows, have been thrown away from the quiver of vain and ruthless people.

The reconstructive hand of the Potter can mend the broken places in any life. Amidst affairs and struggles, needs and incidents, may the peace and calmness of knowing God cause the birth of fresh dreams. But most of all, it lays to rest old fears.

Some friends play at friendship but a true friend sticks closer than one's nearest kin.

Proverbs 18:24 NRSV

Friendship is the last remaining sign of our fleeting childhood dreams. Different from family love, which is not chosen but accepted, this love gradually grows until one day an acquaintance has graduated into a friend. Love is the graduation diploma, whether discussed or hinted.

The world has lost the ability to appreciate the value of a friend. Only occasionally in the course of a lifetime do we meet the kind of friend who is more than an acquaintance. This kind of kindred spirit feels as warm and fitting as an old house shoe, with its personalized contours impressed upon soft fabric for the benefit of weary feet.

The tragedy is that we all yearn for, but seldom acquire, true trust and covenant. The truth is that real relationship is hard work. Your actions express the importance of the other person.

Every relationship undergoes adjustments. We never know the magnitude of a relationship's strength until it is tested by some threatening force. There must be a strong adhesive that can withstand the pressure and not be weakened by outside forces.

But as many as received Him, to them gave He power to become the sons of God, even to them that believe on His name.

John 1:12

My twin sons were playing on the floor with a truck. Later, I noticed that the boys were now running an airplane down an imaginary runway. I asked, "What happened to the truck you were playing with?" They explained, "Daddy, this is a transformer! It can be transformed from what it was before into whatever we want it to be!"

Suddenly I realized that God had made the first transformer! He created man in such a way that He could pull a woman out of him without ever having to reach back into the dust. Out of one creative act God transformed the man into a marriage. Then He transformed the marriage into a family, the family into a society, etc. God never had to reach into the ground again because the power to transform was intrinsically placed into man. God placed certain things in us that must come out. Every word of our personal prophetic destiny is inside us. He has ordained us to be!

*Remove from me reproach and contempt; for I have
kept Thy testimonies.*

Psalm 119:22

Amnon was wicked. He brutally raped his sister Tamar
(see 2 Sam. 13:1-21). He slashed her self-esteem. He
spoiled her integrity. She went into his room a virgin with
a future. When it was over, she was a bleeding, trembling,
crying mass of pain.

Have you ever had anything happen that changed you
forever? Somehow, you survived, yet you knew you
would never be the same. You shout. You sing. You skip.
But when no one is looking, you are still that trembling,
bleeding mass of pain.

Maybe you are in the Church, but you are in trouble.
People move all around you, and you laugh, even enter-
tain them. You are fun to be around. But they don't know.
You can't seem to talk about what happened in your life.

The worst part about it is, after Amnon had abused her, he
didn't even want her. Tamar said, *"What you're doing to
me now is worse than what you did to me at first"* (see 2
Sam. 13:16). When women feel unwanted, it destroys
their sense of esteem and value.

A friend loveth at all times, and a brother is born for adversity.

Proverbs 17:17

Part of what we want from relationships is to know that you won't leave, regardless of what is encountered—even if you discover my worst imperfection! Isn't the real question, "Can I be transparent with you, and be assured that my nudity has not altered your commitment to be my friend?" I know that someone reading this has given up on friendship, with its many expenses and desertions. If you will not believe me, then believe the Word of God. It is possible to attain real abiding friendship.

Even natural blood ties don't always wear as well as heart ties. The Bible says there is a kind of friend that *"sticketh closer than a brother"* (Prov. 18:24b).

The obvious friend is the one who stands by you, honoring and affirming you. A true friend should desire to see me prosper in my marriage, in my finances, and in my health and spirituality. If these virtues are present in the relationship, then we can easily climb over the hurdles of personal imperfection. We transmit through warm exchanges of mutual affection, our celebration of friendship.

Before I formed thee in the belly I knew thee; and before thou camest forth out of the womb I sanctified thee, and I ordained thee a prophet unto the nations.

Jeremiah 1:5

Salvation as it relates to destiny is the God-given power to become what God has eternally decreed you were before the foundation of the world. Grace is God's divine enablement to accomplish predestined purpose. When the Lord tells Paul, *"My grace is sufficient for thee..."* (2 Cor. 12:9), His power is not intimidated by your circumstances. You are empowered by God to accomplish goals that transcend human limitations! It is important that each person God uses realizes that they are able to accomplish what others can not only because God gives them the grace to do so. Problems are not really problems to a person who has the grace to serve in a particular area.

The excellency of our gifts are of God and not of us. He doesn't need nearly as much of our contributions as we think He does. So it is God who works out the internal destinies of men. He gives us the power to become who we are eternally and internally.

So don't be afraid; you are worth more than many sparrows.

Matthew 10:31 NIV

Some of you have gone through divorces, tragedies and adulterous relationships, and you've been left feeling unwanted. It injures something about you that changes how you relate to everyone else for the rest of your life. Amnon didn't even want Tamar afterward. She pleaded with him, "Don't throw me away." Amnon called a servant and said, *"Throw her out."* (see 2 Sam. 13:15).

God knows that the Amnon in your life really does not love you. He's out to abuse you. The servant picked Tamar up, opened the door and threw that victimized woman out. She lay on the ground outside the door with nowhere to go. He told the servant, "Lock the door."

What do you do when you are trapped in a transitory state, neither in nor out? You're left lying at the door, torn up and disturbed, trembling and intimidated. The Bible says she cried. What do you do when you don't know what to do? Filled with regrets, pains, nightmare experiences, seemingly unable to find relief…unable to rise above it, she stayed on the ground. She cried.

She had a coat, a cape of many colors. It was a sign of her virginity and of her future. She was going to give it to her husband one day. She sat there and ripped it up. She was saying, "I have no future. It wasn't just that he took my body. He took my future. He took my esteem and value away."

Two are better than one; because they have a good reward for their labor. For if they fall, the one will lift up his fellow: but woe to him that is alone when he falleth; for he hath not another to help him up.

Ecclesiastes 4:9-10

What we all need is the unique gift of acceptance. Most of us fear the bitter taste of rejection, but perhaps worse than rejection is the naked pain that attacks an exposed heart when a relationship is challenged by some struggle.

Suppose I share my heart with someone who betrays me, and I am wounded again? The distress of betrayal can become a wall that insulates us, but it also isolates us from those around us. There are good reasons for being protective and careful. Love is always a risk. Yet I still suggest that the risk is worth the reward!

Communication becomes needless between people who need no audible speech. Their speech is the soft pat on a shoulder. Their communication is a concerned glance when all is not well with you. If you have ever sunken down into the rich lather of a real covenant relationship, then you are wealthy.

And the Lord said unto Moses, Gather unto Me seventy men of the elders of Israel, whom thou knowest to be the elders of the people, and officers over them; and bring them unto the tabernacle of the congregation, that they may stand there with thee.

Numbers 11:16

The Body of Christ places a great deal of emphasis on the process of mentoring. The concept of mentoring is scriptural and effective; however, many of us have gone to extremes. Instead of teaching young men to pursue God, they are running amuck looking for a man to pour into them.

All men are not mentored as Joshua was—under the firm hand of a strong leader. Some, like Moses, are prepared by the workings of the manifold wisdom of God. They receive mentoring through circumstances that God ordains to accomplish an end result.

Regardless of which describes your ascent to greatness, it is still God who *"worketh in you both to will and to do."* When you understand this, you appreciate the men or the methods God used, but ultimately praise the God whose masterful ability to conduct has crescendoed in the finished product of a man or woman of God.

Since thou wast precious in My sight, thou hast been honorable, and I have loved thee: therefore will I give men for thee, and people for thy life.

Isaiah 43:4

There's a call out in the Spirit for hurting women. "I've seen you bent over and the aftereffects of what happened to you. I've seen you at your worst moment. I still want you." God has not changed His mind. God loves with an everlasting love.

When Jesus encountered the infirm woman of Luke 13, He called to her. There may have been many fine women present that day, but the Lord didn't call them forward. He reached around all of them and found that crippled woman in the back. He called forth the wounded, hurting woman with a past. He issued the Spirit's call to those who had their value and self-esteem destroyed by the intrusion of vicious circumstances.

The infirm woman must have thought, "He wants me. I'm frayed and torn, but He wants me. I have been through trouble. I have been through this trauma, but He wants me." Perhaps she thought no one would ever want her again, but Jesus wanted her. He had a plan.

And let us consider one another to provoke unto love and to good works.

Hebrews 10:24

Children understand the rich art of relationship. They are often angry, but their anger quickly dissipates in the glaring sunshine of a fresh opportunity to laugh and jest a day away. The hearts of most adults, however, have been blackened by unforgiveness. They will hold a club of remembered infractions against one another for long periods of time, perhaps for a lifetime. There is a vacancy in the hearts of most men that causes them to be narrow and superficial. This vacancy is the vast gap between casual relationships and intimate attachments. It is the gift of friendship that should fill the gap between these wide designated points of human relationship.

Since there is no blood to form the basis of relativity between friends, the bond must exist through some other mode of reality. A commonality is needed to anchor the relationship of two individuals. However, this bond may exist in an area that outsiders would never understand, but thank God their confusion doesn't dilute the intensity of admiration that exists between true friends. Dare to be a friend!

God exalted Him to His own right hand as Prince and Savior that He might give repentance and for- giveness of sins to Israel.

Acts 5:31 NIV

Change is a gift from God. It is given to the person who finds himself too far removed from what he feels destiny has ordained for him. Don't assume that real change occurs without struggle and prayer.

The Bible calls change repentance. Repentance is God's gift to a struggling heart who wants to find himself. Without the Holy Spirit's help you can search and search and still not find repentance. The Lord will show the place of repentance only to those who hunger and thirst after righteousness. The Spirit of God can lead you into a place of renewal that, on your own, you would not find. I believe it was this kind of grace that made John Newton record, "It was grace that taught my heart to fear and grace my fears relieved. How precious did that grace appear the hour I first believed" ("Amazing Grace," early American melody). When God gives you the grace to make changes that you know you couldn't do with your own strength, it becomes precious to you.

And let us consider one another to provoke unto love and to good works.

Hebrews 10:24

The extent of damage that mortal men can do to the upright is limited by the purposes of God. What a privilege it is to know and understand this in your heart. It destroys the constant paranoia that restricts many of us from exploring possible friendships and covenant relationships. Any time you make an investment, there is the possibility of a loss. But there is a difference between being hurt and being altered or destroyed.

You belong to God, and He watches over you every day. He monitors your affairs, and acts as your protection. Sometimes He opens doors (we always get excited about God opening doors). But the same God who opens doors also closes doors. I am, perhaps, more grateful for the doors He has closed in my life than I am for the ones He has opened. Had I been allowed to enter some of the doors He closed, I would surely have been destroyed! God doesn't intend for every relationship to flourish. There are some human cliques and social groups in which He doesn't want you to be included!

And now, Lord, what wait I for? my hope is in Thee.

Psalm 39:7

And, behold, there was a woman which had a spirit of infirmity eighteen years...And He laid His hands on her: and immediately she was made straight, and glorified God.

Luke 13:11-13

If you can identify with the feelings of this infirm woman, then know that He's waiting on you. He sees your struggling and He knows your pain. He knows what happened to you 18 years ago or even last week. With patience He waits for you. Jesus says to the hurting and crippled, "I want you enough to wait for you to hobble your way back home."

When the infirm woman came to Jesus, He proclaimed her freedom. She stood erect for the first time in 18 years. When you come to Jesus, He will cause you to stand in His strength. Part of your recovery is to learn how to stand up and live in the "now" of life instead of the "then" of yesterday. You will know how important you are to Him. Realize that you are the daughter of a king. Your Father is the King.

And to the angel of the church in Philadelphia write; These things saith He that is holy, He that is true, He that hath the key of David, He that openeth, and no man shutteth; and shutteth, and no man openeth.

Revelation 3:7

The letter to the Philadelphia church, the church of brotherly love, basically ends with the words, "I am the One who closes doors." The art to surviving painful moments is living in the "yes" zone. We need to learn to respond to God with a yes when the doors are open, and a yes when they are closed. Our prayer must be:

I trust Your decisions, Lord; and I know that if this relationship is good for me, You will allow it to continue. I know that if the door is closed, it is also for my good. So I say "yes" to You as I go into this relationship. I appreciate brotherly love, and I still say "yes" if You close the door.

This is the epitome of a trust that is seldom achieved, but is to be greatly sought after. In so doing, you will be able to savor companionship without the fear of reprisal!

For ye know how that afterward, when he would have inherited the blessing, he was rejected: for he found no place of repentance, though he sought it carefully with tears.

Hebrews 12:17

Brother Esau sought for the place of repentance and could not secure it. To be transformed is to be changed. If you are not moving into your divine purpose, you desperately need to repent.... If God wants you to change, it is because He wants you to be prepared for what He desires to do next in your life. Get ready; the best is yet to come.

In Romans 12:2 we are instructed not to be conformed to this world. Literally, it says we are not to be conformed to the same *pattern* of this world.... We are to avoid using those standards as a pattern for our progress. On a deeper level God is saying, "Do not use the same pattern of the world to measure success or to establish character and values." The term "world" in Greek is *aion* (Strong's #G165), which refers to ages. Do not allow the pattern of the times you are in to become the pattern that shapes your inward person.

I waited patiently for the Lord; and He inclined unto me, and heard my cry. He brought me up also out of an horrible pit, out of the miry clay, and set my feet upon a rock, and established my goings.

Psalm 40:1-3

I proclaim to the abused: There is a healing going into your spirit right now. I speak life to you. I speak deliverance to you. I speak restoration to you. All in the mighty name of Jesus, in the invincible, all-powerful, everlasting name of Jesus. I proclaim victory to you. You will recover the loss you suffered at the hands of your abuser. You will get back every stolen item. God will heal that broken twig. He will rebuild your self-esteem, your self-respect, and your integrity.

The anointing of God is reaching out to you. He calls you forth to set you free. When you reach out to Him and allow the Holy Spirit to have His way, His anointing is present to deliver you. Demons will tremble. Satan wants to keep you at the door, but never let you enter. He wants to keep you down. Now his power is broken in your life.

And we know that all things work together for good for them that love God, to them who are the called according to His purpose.

Romans 8:28

If no good can come out of a relationship or situation, then God will not allow it. There must be an inner awareness within your heart, a deep knowledge that God is in control and that He is able to reverse the adverse. When we believe in His sovereignty, we can overcome every humanly induced trial because we realize that they are divinely permitted. He orchestrates them in such a way that the things that could have paralyzed us only motivate us.

Even in the most harmonious of relationships there are injuries and adversity. If you live in a cocoon, you will miss all the different levels of love God has for you. God allows different people to come into your life to accomplish His purposes. Your friends are ultimately the ones who will help you become all that God wants you to be in Him. When you consider it in that light, you have many friends—some of them expressed friends, and some implied friends.

To be made new in the attitude of your minds.
Ephesians 4:23 NIV

Many individuals in the Body of Christ are perse-vering without progressing. They wrestle with areas that have been conformed to the world instead of transformed. This is particularly true of we Pente-costals who often emphasize the gifts of the Spirit and exciting services. It is imperative that, while we keep our mode of expression, we understand that transfor-mation doesn't come from inspiration! Transformation takes place in the mind.

The Bible teaches that we are to be renewed by the trans-forming of our minds (see Rom. 12:2; Eph. 4:23). Only the Holy Spirit knows how to renew the mind. The strug-gle we have inside us is with our self-perception. Gener-ally our perception of ourselves is affected by those around us. Our early opinion of ourselves is deeply affected by the opinions of the authoritative figures in our formative years. If our parents tend to neglect or ignore us, it tears at our self-worth. Eventually, though, we mature to the degree where we can walk in the light of our own self-image, without it being diluted by the contributions of others.

> *To appoint unto them that mourn in Zion, to give unto them beauty for ashes, the oil of joy for mourning, the garment of praise for the spirit of heaviness; that they might be called trees of righteousness, the planting of the Lord, that He might be glorified.*
>
> *Isaiah 61:3*

The Church is a place where you can come broken and disgusted, and be healed, delivered, and set free in the name of Jesus.

Jesus said, *"The Spirit of the Lord is upon Me, because He hath anointed Me to preach the gospel to the poor; He hath sent Me to heal the brokenhearted, to preach deliverance to the captives, and recovering of sight to the blind, to set at liberty them that are bruised"* (Luke 4:18).

You may have thought that you would never rejoice again. God declares that you can have freedom in Him—now! The joy that He brings can be restored to your soul. He identifies with your pain and suffering. He knows what it is like to suffer abuse at the hands of others. Yet He proclaims joy and strength. He will give you the garment of praise instead of the spirit of heaviness.

The Lord is on my side; I will not fear: what can man do unto me?

Psalm 118:6

God has used certain "friends" and their negativity to accomplish His will for our lives. Now, because our ultimate goal is to please Him, we must widen our definition of friendship to include the betrayer if his betrayal ushered us into the next step of God's plan for our lives.

There are some friends who were actually instrumental in my blessing, although they never really embraced or affirmed me as a person! They played a crucial part in my well-being. These kinds of "friends" are the "Judas sector" that exists in the life of every child of God.

Every child of God not only has, but also desperately needs, a "Judas" to carry out certain aspects of divine providence in his life! Although Peter was certainly more amiable and admirable, Judas was the one God selected to usher in the next step of the process. Sometimes your friends are the ones who can cause you the most pain. They wound you and betray you, but through their betrayal God's will can be executed in your life.

For we are His workmanship, created in Christ Jesus unto good works, which God hath before ordained that we should walk in them.

Ephesians 2:9b

Jesus knew who He was. The Lord wants to help you realize who you are and what you are graced to do. To ask someone to define you without first knowing the answer yourself is dangerous. When you understand that He is the only One who really knows you, then you pursue Him with fierceness and determination. Pursue Him!

God knows who we are and how we are to attain our calling. This knowledge, locked up in the counsel of God's omniscience, is the basis of our pursuit, and it is the release of that knowledge that brings immediate transformation. He knows the hope or the goal of our calling. He is not far removed from us; He reveals Himself to people who seek Him. The finders are the seekers. The door is opened only to the knockers and the gifts are given to the askers! (See Luke 11:9.) Initiation is our responsibility. Whosoever hungers and thirsts shall be filled. Remember, in every crisis He is never far from the seeker!

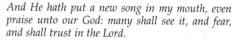

And He hath put a new song in my mouth, even praise unto our God: many shall see it, and fear, and shall trust in the Lord.

Psalm 40:3

He will restore to you that which the cankerworm and the locust ate up (see Joel 2:25). He said, "I'm going to give it back to you." Maybe you wrestle with guilt. You feel so dirty. You've been misused and abused. The devil keeps bringing up to you your failures of the past.

I always tended to have a ministry of mercy. Perhaps it is because I've had my own pain. When you have suffered, it makes you able to relate to other people's pain. Sometimes when I minister, I find myself fighting back tears.

Once you have called out to Him, you can lift up your hands in praise. No matter what you have suffered, you can hold up your head. Regardless of who has hurt you, hold up your head! Forget how many times you've been married. Put aside those who mistreated you. It doesn't matter who you were. You can't change where you have been, but you can change where you are going.

What shall we then say to these things? If God be for us, who can be against us?

Romans 8:31

Judas was no mistake. He was handpicked and selected. His role was crucial to the death and resurrection of Christ. No one helped Christ reach His goal like Judas. If God allowed certain types of people to come into our lives, they would hinder us from His divine purpose. A seasoned heart has been exercised by the tragedies of life. It has reduced and controlled the fatty feelings and emotions that cause us to always seek those whose actions tickle our ears.

We all want to be surrounded by a friend like John, whose loving head lay firmly on Jesus' breast. We may long for the protective instincts of a friend like Peter, who stood ready to attack every negative force that would come against Jesus. In his misdirected love, Peter even withstood Jesus to His face over His determination to die for mankind. But the truth of the matter is, Jesus could have accomplished His goal without Peter, James, or John; but without Judas He would never have reached the hope of His calling!

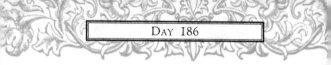

That He might sanctify and cleanse it with the washing of water by the word.

Ephesians 5:26

Transforming truths are brought forth through the birth canal of our diligence in seeking His face. David said, *"In Thy presence is fullness of joy"* (Ps. 16:11b). The answer is in the Presence of God, not man! A renewing word will change your mind about your circumstance. Just when the enemy thinks he has you, transform before his very eyes!

No matter who left his impression upon you, God's Word prevails! The obstacles of past scars can be overcome by present truths. Your deliverance will not start in your circumstances; it evolves out of your mentality. As the Word of God waxes greater, the will of men becomes weaker. Turn the faucet of God's Word on high and ease your mind down into the water of profound truth. Wash away every limitation and residue of past obstacles and transform into the renewed person you were created to become. Whenever someone tells you what you can't do or be, or what you can't get or attain, tell them, *"I can do all things through Christ who strengthens me"* (see Phil. 4:13).

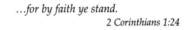

...for by faith ye stand.

2 Corinthians 1:24

The Holy Spirit is calling for the broken, infirm women to come to Jesus. He will restore and deliver. How do we come to Jesus? We come to His Body, the Church. It is in the Church that we can hear the Word of God. The Church gives us strength and nourishment. The Church is to be the place where we share our burdens and allow others to help us with them. The Spirit calls; the burdened need only heed the call.

There are three tenses of faith! When Lazarus died, Martha, his sister, said, *"Lord, if You would have been here, my brother would not have died."* This is historical faith. Its view is digressive. Then when Jesus said, *"Lazarus will live again,"* his sister replied, *"I know he will live in the resurrection."* This is futuristic faith. It is progressive. Martha says, *"But even now You have the power to raise him up again."* (See John 11:21-27.)

I feel like Martha. Even now, after all you've been through, God has the power to raise you up again! This is the present tense of faith. Walk into your newness even now.

It is good for me that I have been afflicted; that I might learn Thy statutes.

Psalm 119:71

What happens when friendship takes an unusual form? Did you know that God, our ultimate Friend, sometimes manipulates the actions of our enemies to cause them to work as friends in order to accomplish His will in our lives? God can bless you through the worst of relationships! That is why we must learn how to accept even the relationships that seem to be painful or negative. The time, effort, and pain we invest in them is not wasted because God knows how to make adversity feed destiny into your life!

I cannot stop your hurts from coming; neither can I promise that everyone who sits at the table with you is loyal. But I can suggest that the sufferings of success give us direction and build character within us. Finally, you find the grace to reevaluate your enemies and realize that many of them were friends in disguise. As God heals what hurt you have, remember that betrayal is only sweetened when it is accompanied by survival. Live on, my friend, live on!

*The Lord possessed me in the beginning of His way,
before His works of old....Then I was by Him, as
one brought up with Him: and I was daily His
delight, rejoicing always before Him.*

Proverbs 8:22,30

The streaming fount of holy blood that flows from the gaping wounds of my loving Savior has draped my wretchedness in His holiness. He has covered me like Boaz covered Ruth. His blood also has covered me like a warm blanket on a cold night. I found my past nestled beneath His omnipresent banner of love and concern, taking the chill out of my life and removing the stiffness from my heart. When I had no one to snuggle close to, He became my eternal companion—always seeking out what is best for me and bringing before me great and mighty things.

I confess that I often used to resist loneliness. I filled my life with work and with people who meant me no good at all. At that time, I would rather have filled my life with noise than run the risk of total silence. How foolish of me not to note the difference between being alone and being lonely.

When I was a child, I spoke as a child, I understood as a child, I thought as a child; but when I became a man, I put away childish things. For now we see in a mirror, dimly, but then face to face. Now I know in part, but then I shall know just as I also am known.

1 Corinthians 13:11-12 NKJV

Attitudes affect the way we live our lives. A good attitude can bring success. A poor attitude can bring destruction. An attitude results from perspective. Everyone seems to have a different perspective. It comes from the way we look at life which is often determined by our history.

The events of the past can cause us to have an outlook or perspective on life that is less than God's perspective. The little girl who was abused learns to defend herself by not trusting men. This attitude of defensiveness often stretches into adulthood. If we have protected ourselves a certain way in the past with some measure of success, then it is natural to continue that pattern throughout life. Unfortunately, we often need to learn how to look past our perspective and change our attitudes.

*Now also when I am old and greyheaded, O God,
forsake me not; until I showed Thy strength unto
this generation, and Thy power to every one that is
to come.*

Psalm 71:18

I recently had the privilege of entertaining my 90-year-old grandmother, whose robust frame has deteriorated to just a mere shadow of its former presence.

This was the Trojan-like woman who had worked her way through college doing laundry, studying in the wee hours of the night. This was the Mississippi matron who captured a teaching degree in the middle of her life. Now she had come to the setting of the sun.

I could see that sun burning behind her leathery skin and glazed eyes. Age had somehow smothered her need to talk, and she would lapse into long periods of silence that left me clamoring foolishly through asinine conversations. Whenever I asked her if she was all right, she would respond affirmatively and assure me that she was greatly enjoying my company. Then she would flee into the counsel of her own thoughts and come out at intervals to play with me, with some humorous statement that would remind me of her earlier years.

Behold, I go forward, but He is not there; and backward, but I cannot perceive Him: on the left hand, where He doth work, but I cannot behold, Him; He hideth Himself on the right hand, that I cannot see Him.

Job 23:8-9

There are times when it is difficult to understand God's methods. There are moments when discerning His will is frustrating. Perhaps we have these moments because we haven't been given all the information we need to ascertain His ways as well as His acts. Many times we learn more in retrospect than we do while in the thick of the struggle. I can look at my past and see that the hand of the Lord has been on me all my life. Yet there were times when I felt completely alone and afraid. Even Jesus once cried out, *"Eli, Eli, lama sabachthani? that is to say, My God, My God, why hast Thou forsaken Me?"* (Matt. 27:46b) Suspended on the Cross with a bloody, beaten body, He was questioning the acts of God—but He never questioned His relationship with Him. Jesus says in essence, "I don't understand why, but You are still My God!"

The lamp of the Lord searches the spirit of a man; it searches out his inmost being.

Proverbs 20:27 NIV

As I pondered my 90-year-old grandmother's behavior and her silent, Indian-like demeanor, I realized that her silence was not boredom. It was, first of all, the mark of someone who has learned how to be alone. It reflected the hours she had spent sitting in a rocking chair, entertaining herself with her own thoughts, and reconciling old accounts that brought the past into balance before the books were presented to the Master Himself. She was at peace, with the kind of peace that comes from a firm faith and deep resolution.

I am rewarded with a friendly reminder from a loving God who speaks through the glazed eyes of an aged relative, telling me to relax and enjoy life. It was there that I made two commitments in my own mind, as my grandmother smiled and gazed out of a window as if she were looking at Heaven itself. I committed to a renewed faith and trust in the ableness of God. The other commitment I made may seem strange, but I promised to spend more time with myself, to warm myself at the fire of my own thoughts and smile with the contentments of the riches contained therein.

> *You were taught, with regard to your former way*
> *of life, to put off your old self, which is being cor-*
> *rupted by its deceitful desires; to be made new in*
> *the attitude of your minds; and to put on the new*
> *self, created to be like God in true righteousness*
> *and holiness.*
>
> *Ephesians 4:22-24 NIV*

Today, many of us have things we need to be separated from or burdens we need lifted. We can function to a certain point under a load, but we can't function as effectively as we would if the thing was lifted off of us. Perhaps some of you right now have things that are burdening you down.

It is God's intention that we be set free from the loads we carry. Many people live in codependent relationships. Others are anesthetized to their problems because they have had them so long. Perhaps you have become so accustomed to having a problem that even when you get a chance to be delivered, you find it hard to let it go. Problems can become like a security blanket.

Before you get out of trouble, straighten out your attitude. Until your attitude is corrected, you can't be corrected.

Finally, brethren, whatsoever things are true, whatsoever things are honest, whatsoever things are just, whatsoever things are pure, whatsoever things are lovely, whatsoever things are of good report; if there be any virtue, and if there be any praise, think on these things.

Philippians 4:8

We must understand that modern medicine can heal many afflictions of the body, and can even treat the tumors that sometimes attach themselves to the brain, but only God Himself can heal the mind. Do you know that many times your thoughts need to be healed? Your thoughts are often the product of damaged emotions, traumatic events, and vicious opinions forced upon you by the bodacious personalities of domineering people who continually feel it necessary to express their opinions about you.

You do have control over your thoughts. You must choose what you are going to meditate upon. Choose carefully, though, for you will ultimately become whatever it is you meditate upon. The enemy knows this, so when he wants to destroy your morality, he doesn't start with an act; he starts with a thought. A thought is a seed that, if not aborted, will produce offspring somewhere in your life.

As the hart panteth after the water brooks, so panteth my soul after Thee, O God. My soul thirsteth for God, for the living God: when shall I come and appear before God? My tears have been my meat day and night, while they continually say unto me, Where is thy God? When I remember these things, I pour out my soul in me: for I had gone with the multitude, I went with them to the house of God, with the voice of joy and praise, with a multitude that kept holyday.

Psalm 42:1-4

The search for God is a primary step into worship. We never search for anything we don't value. There are millions of people who seem to live their lives without noticing that something is missing. The very fact that we search for Him indicates that He has become essential to us. The word "worship" stems from the term *worth-ship*. It expresses the worth of an object. The kind of intensity that causes an individual to pursue the invisible in spite of all the visible distractions is a result of need. If we didn't need Him desperately, we could easily be satisfied with carnal things.

*Let the words of my mouth, and the meditation of
my heart, be acceptable in Thy sight, O Lord, my
strength, and my redeemer.*

Psalm 19:14

You must quickly cast down an evil thought. "Push
the remote control" before it drains away your commitment to excellence and leaves you crying in the valley of regret. The real temptation to entertain thoughts is
in the privacy of the mind. Who will know what you
really think? You can smile at people and never disclose
your innermost thoughts.

I always laugh when I see people act as though they have
conquered the battle with the mind. I've asked people in
my services, "Which of you would be comfortable with
having everything that comes to mind played on a television screen for all of your Christian friends to watch? Or
which of you would like to have all our thoughts through
the week played over the loudspeaker at church next
Sunday?" I'm sure I don't have to tell you, they all put
their hands down.

Our mind is a private battleground that can easily
become a secret place for contamination, lust, fear, low
self-esteem, and God only knows what else!

Therefore, since Christ suffered in His body, arm yourselves also with the same attitude, because he who has suffered in his body is done with sin. As a result, he does not live the rest of his earthly life for evil human desires, but rather for the will of God.

1 Peter 4:1-2 NIV

Why should we put up all the ramps and rails for the handicapped if we can heal them? You want everyone to make an allowance for your problem, but your problem needs to make an allowance for God and to humble itself to the point where you don't need special help. I'm addressing the emotional baggage that keeps us from total health. You cannot expect the whole human race to move over because you had a bad childhood. They will not do it. You may have trouble with relationships because people don't accommodate your hang-up.

Christ wants to separate you from the source of your bitterness until it no longer gives you the kind of attitude that makes you a carrier of pain. Your attitude affects your situation—your attitude, not other people's attitude about you. Your attitude will give you life or death.

Thou knowest my downsitting and mine uprising,
Thou understandest my thought afar off.

Psalm 139:2

We shouldn't allow our minds to collect scum and clutter without any regard to cleaning and renewing the mind. Here are several reasons not to do that.

First, a certain Someone does know what we think. Second, we need to continually purge our thoughts because we become what we think. Third, we need to renew our minds daily in God's presence, for I believe that as we hear the thoughts of God, His thinking becomes increasingly contagious. Let's deal with the first of these three.

God sits in the living quarters of the minds of men and beholds their thoughts. He knows our thoughts afar off (see Ps. 139:2). If we are serious about entertaining His presence, we cannot lie to Him—He sees us from the inside out.

We must be honest and admit to Him: I know that if it were not for Your mercy, I would be guilty of the very things for which I have disdained others. I praise You for loving me, in spite of all You know about me.

*But without faith it is impossible to please Him:
for he that cometh to God must believe that He is,
and that He is a rewarder of them that diligently
seek Him.*

Hebrews 11:6

There are no manuals that instruct us step by step as to the proper way to seek the Lord. There are no rules—just that we seek Him with our whole hearts.

My friend, don't be afraid to stretch out your hands to reach after Him. Cry after Him. Whatever you do, do not allow this moment to pass you by!

Like groping fingers extended in the night trying to compensate for a darkened vision, we feel after God. We feel after His will and His ways. I'm amazed at all the people who seem to always know everything God is saying about everything. In their hymn, Ray Palmer and Lowell Mason wrote, "My faith looks up to thee, Oh lamb of Calvary, savior divine." My faith looks up because my eyes can't always see. On the other hand, there is a healthy reaction that occurs in blindness; our senses become keener as we exercise areas that we wouldn't normally need.

It is of the Lord's mercies that we are not consumed, because His compassions fail not. They are new every morning: great is Thy faithfulness.

Lamentations 3:22-23

Forgive me for condemning and judging anybody else. I know that if it were not for Your mercy, I would be guilty of the very things for which I have disdained others. Help me not to be hypocritical.

This kind of prayer and confession enhances your relationship with God as you begin to realize that you *were* saved by grace; you *are* saved by grace; and you *will* be saved by grace! Knowing this, how can you not be grateful? You know that He loves you so much that He stays in the house you haven't fully cleaned. He hates the acts; He despises the thoughts; but He loves the thinker.

God knows all our business and all our thoughts parade around naked before His scrutinizing eyes. We need a high priest for all the garbage and information that the Holy Spirit is privy to, yet others would never know. What greater compassion can be displayed than how God, through Christ, can be touched by how I feel.

But Jesus turned him about, and when he saw her, he said, Daughter, be of good comfort; thy faith hath made thee whole. And the woman was made whole from that hour.

Matthew 9:22

One of the greatest deliverances people can ever experience in life is to have their attitude delivered. It doesn't do you any good to be delivered financially if your attitude doesn't change. I can give you $5,000, but if your attitude, your mental perspective, doesn't change, you will be broke in a week because you'll lose it again. The problem is not how much you have, it's what you do with what you have. If you can change your attitude, you might have only $50, but you'll take that $50 and learn how to get $5 million.

When God comes to heal, He wants to heal your emotions also. Sometimes all we pray about is our situation. We bring God our shopping list of desires. Fixing circumstances is like applying a Band-Aid, though. Healing attitudes set people free to receive wholeness.

You might think that the greatest deliverance is physical deliverance. Another deliverance that was even greater— that of an attitude change.

For as he thinketh in his heart, so is he.

Proverbs 23:7

If no one knows what we think, why shouldn't we allow our minds to collect scum and clutter without any regard to cleaning and renewing the mind? Here is one good reason.

We need to continually purge our thoughts because we become what we think. It is not just the lust that we must clean out, but also low self-esteem, pride, arrogance, jealousy, and much more. The mind is the "placenta" of the spirit man. It holds and nurtures the seeds it has been impregnated with until their time of delivery. If you don't want the child that that seed of thought produces, your only recourse is to abort before it is carried to full term.

If you don't want depression, why do you continue to regurgitate those same sickening thoughts that lead you into emotional depravity? You don't need a famous minister to lay hands on you to win the battle over your mind! Generally speaking, demonstrations of public power seldom accomplish deliverance from mental images. You need the inner discipline required of all disciples to resist evil thoughts before they become evidenced in your life.

Ask, and it shall be given you; seek, and ye shall find; knock, and it shall be opened unto you. For every one that asketh receiveth; and he that seeketh findeth; and to him that knocketh it shall be opened.

Matthew 7:7-8

Searching releases answers. Many things available to us will not be found without an all-out search. Seeking God also takes focus. This search has to be what the police call an A.P.B—an "all points bulletin." The entire department is asked to seek the same thing. Thus our search can't be a distracted, half-hearted curiosity. There must be something to produce a unified effort: body, soul, and spirit—all points—seeking the same thing. There is a blessing waiting for us. It will require an A.P.B. to bring it into existence, but it will be worth attaining. Who knows what God will release if we go on an all-out God-hunt.

The crucial times that arise in our lives require more than good advice. We need a Word from God. There are moments when we need total seclusion. We come home from work, turn off the telephone, and lie before God for a closer connection.

They said, "Teacher, we know that You are an honest man and that You teach the truth about God's way. You are not afraid of what other people think about You, because You pay no attention to who they are."

Matthew 22:16b NCV

The mind is continually being reconstructed by the Holy Spirit to enable you to soar above your past.

Christ has a balanced mind. He doesn't suffer from low self-esteem. He "thought it not robbery" to be equal with God (see Phil. 2:5-7). For Him, being equal with God was and is a reality. That might seem a little extreme for you and me. He was comfortable with His exaltation. He didn't allow opinions of other men to determine who He "thought" He was. His inner perception was fixed.

The miracle of His strength is that, unlike most people who are that strong about their inner worth, Christ Jesus did not wrestle with arrogance. He knew who He was, yet He *"made Himself of no reputation"* (Phil. 2:7a). When you have healthy thoughts about your own identity, it frees you from the need to impress other people. Their opinion ceases to be the shrine where you worship!

If you do not stand firm in your faith, you will not stand at all.

Isaiah 7:9b NIV

The Lord is your defense. You do not have to defend yourself. When God has delivered you, do not stop what you're doing to answer your accusers. Continue to bless His name, because you do not want your attitude to become defensive. When you have been through difficult times, you cannot afford to play around with moods and attitudes. Depression and defensiveness may make you vulnerable to the devil.

When you get to the point that you quit defending yourself or attacking others, you open up a door for the Lord to fight for you.

When you're in trouble, God will reach into the mess and pull you out. However, you must be strong enough not to let people drag you back into it. Once God unleashes you, don't let anyone trap you into some religious fight. Keep praising Him. The more people criticize you, the more you should just stand and keep believing God. God is trying to get you to a place of faith. He is trying to deliver you from an attitude of negatives.

Know ye not that ye are the temple of God, and that the Spirit of God dwelleth in you? If any man defile the temple of God, him shall God destroy; for the temple of God is holy, which temple ye are.

1 Corinthians 3:16-17

Most of us come to the Lord damaged. We're dead spiritually, damaged emotionally, and decaying physically. When He saved you, He quickened, or made alive, your dead spirit. He also promised you a new body. Then He began the massive renovation necessary to repair your damaged thoughts about life, about others, and about yourself—here come all types of nails, saws, levels, bricks, and blocks.

We all need the Lord to help us with ourselves. We came to Him as condemned buildings, and He reopened the places that satan thought would never be inhabited. The Holy Spirit moved in, but He brought His hammers and His saw with Him.

While we dress and smell nice outwardly, people do not hear the constant hammering and sawing going on inwardly, as the Lord works within us, trying desperately to meet a deadline and present us as a newly constructed masterpiece fit for the Master's use.

Seek ye the Lord while He may be found, call ye upon Him while He is near: let the wicked forsake his way, and the unrighteous man his thoughts: and let him return unto the Lord, and He will have mercy upon him; and to our God, for He will abundantly pardon.

Isaiah 55:6-7

Unfortunately, it generally takes devastation on a business level to make most men commit more of their interest in relationships. Job probably could have reached out to his children for comfort, but he had lost them too. His marriage had deteriorated to the degree that Job said his wife abhorred his breath (see Job 19:17). Then he also became ill. Have you ever gone through a time in your life when you felt you had been jinxed? Everything that could go wrong, did! Frustration turns into alienation. So now what? Will you use this moment to seek God or to brood over your misfortune? With the right answer, you could turn the jail into a church!

If the storms keep coming, the lightning flashes, and the thunder thumps, what matters is keeping the waters out of the inside. Keep that stuff out of your spirit!

For My thoughts are not your thoughts, neither are your ways My ways, saith the Lord. For as the heavens are higher than the earth, so are My ways higher than your ways, and My thoughts than your thoughts.

Isaiah 55:8-9

We need to renew our minds daily in God's presence, for I believe that as we hear the thoughts of God, His thinking becomes increasingly contagious. It is so important that we have a relationship with Him. His Word becomes a lifeline thrown to a man who would otherwise drown in the swirling whirlpool of his own thoughts.

Job said that he esteemed God's Word more than his necessary food (see Job 23:12). As for me, God is my counselor. He talks with me about my deepest, darkest issues; He comforts the raging tide of my fears and inhibitions. What would we be if He would wax silent and cease to guide us through this perilous maze of mental mania? It is His soft words that turn away the wrath of our nagging memories. If He speaks to me, His words become symphonies of enlightenment falling like soft rain on a tin roof. They give rest and peace.

I will bless the Lord at all time: His praise shall continually be in my mouth. My soul shall make her boast in the Lord: the humble shall hear thereof, and be glad.

Psalm 34:1-2

And He laid His hands on her: and immediately she was made straight, and glorified God. And the ruler of the synagogue answered with indignation…. The Lord then answered him, and said, Thou hypocrite…. And ought not this woman, being a daughter of Abraham, whom Satan hath bound, lo, these eighteen years, be loosed from this bond on the sabbath day?

Luke 13:13-16

God must have healed this woman's emotions also because she kept praising Him instead of paying attention to the quarrel of the religious folks around her. She could have easily fallen into negative thinking. Instead, she praised God.

The Lord wants to speak a word of faith to you. He wants to set you free from every power that has kept you in bondage. In order for that to be received in your spirit, you must allow Him to come in and instill faith. The emotional walls that surround us have to come down.

For the vision is yet for an appointed time, but at the end it shall speak, and not lie: though it tarry, wait for it; because it will surely come, it will not tarry.

Habakkuk 2:3

Quite honestly, there are moments when life feels like it has all the purpose of gross insanity. These are the times that try men's hearts. These are the times when we seek answers!

Like a desperate sailor trying to plug a leaking ship, Job frantically cast back and forth in his mind, looking for some shred, some fragment of hope. Exasperated, he sullenly sat in the stupor of his condition and sadly confessed, *"Behold, I go forward, but He is not there"* (Job 23:8a). "I can't find Him where I thought He would be." Have you ever told yourself that the storm would be over soon? And the sun came and the sun left, and still the same rains beat vehemently against the ship. It almost feels as if God missed His appointment. You thought He would move by now! Remember, dear friend, God doesn't synchronize His clock by your little mortal watch. He has a set time to bless you; just hold on.

*Surely He shall deliver thee from the snare of the
fowler, and from the noisome pestilence.*

Psalm 91:3

God's Word will accomplish what it is sent out to do.
God says, "I won't stop in the middle of the job. I
will not give up on you. I will keep hammering until you
are balanced in your thinking and whole in your judg-
ments." No one would ever believe that you were initially
in such a deplorable state! He covers you with His precious blood even while His Word works on you.

Most of the time God delivers us (or is in the process of
delivering us) while we maintain a veil of secrecy to protect our reputations and public perceptions. Secular
scholars would be appalled if they knew how many of us
were in serious trouble when we came to our wit's end
and submitted to the redemptive work of the Lord. It was
He who delivered us out from under the stress and the
strain of our crises. His power forces open the fowler's
snare that entrapped the mind. His Word gives us the
grace to seize the opportunity to escape and go on with
our lives!

But now, O Lord, Thou art our father; we are the clay, and Thou our potter; and we all are the work of Thy hand.

Isaiah 64:8

Where is the God who sent an earthquake into the valley of dry bones and put them together? (See Ezekiel 37.) Or where is the God of the clay, who remolds the broken places and mends the jagged edge? (See Isaiah 64:8.) The God we seek is never far away. The issue is not so much His presence as it is my perception. Many times deliverance doesn't cost God one action. Deliverance comes when my mind accepts His timing and purpose in my life.

In my hours of crises, many times I found myself searching for the place of rest rather than for the answer. If I can find God, my needs become insignificant in the light of His presence. What is a problem if God is there? Do you realize the power of God's presence? I hear many people speak about the acts of God, but have you ever considered the mere presence of God? He doesn't have to do anything but be there, and it is over!

Thou has proved mine heart; Thou hast visited me in the night; Thou hast tried me, and shalt find nothing; I am purposed that my mouth shall not transgress.

Psalm 17:3

There is a strong tie between thought and action. Some time ago, when we discovered the power of our words, we began to teach Christians to speak positively. That is good. The only problem is, we were thinking one thing while the mouth was confessing something else. The results were not rewarding.

The Scriptures tell us that *"with the heart man believeth unto righteousness; and with the mouth confession is made unto salvation"* (Rom. 10:10). There is a strong tie between what is believed and what is confessed. Your thoughts have to align with your confession—otherwise your house is divided against itself! Even God works out of the reservoir of His own thoughts. He does not consider what others think about you. Some of those people don't even believe in God. Nevertheless, He doesn't work out of their thoughts; He works out of His own! Quit trying to change the minds of other people—change your own. Your works will come out of the healing of your thoughts!

The Lord is good. His love is forever, and His loyalty goes on and on.

Psalm 100:5 NCV

Love is eternal. It is not limited by time. When you commit yourself to loving someone, you make that commitment to all the person is. You are who you are because of your history. For me, that means I love my wife and who she has become. But in order for me to love her effectively, she must allow me into her history.

Many couples in a relationship argue over relatively insignificant things. Often the reason these things are important is one or the other is reminded of a past event. How can one person love another if he or she doesn't know the other person's history?

Thousands walk in fear. The Church can give them strength. Thousands have built a wall around them because they do not trust anyone else. The Church can help its members learn to trust one another. Thousands are codependent and get their value from a relationship with another person. The Church can point to God's love as the source for self-worth. We are not valuable because we love God; we are valuable because He loves us.

No weapon that is formed against thee shall prosper; and every tongue that shall rise against thee in judgment thou shalt condemn.

Isaiah 54:17a

If we could talk to the three Hebrews who survived the fiery furnace, perhaps they would describe their experience with the Lord in the midst of the fire in this manner:

"The fire was all over us. Our ropes were ablaze, but our skin seemed undisturbed. Then something moved over in the smoke and ashes. We were not alone! His presence brought comfort in the fire. It was His presence that created protection in the midst of the crisis. Now, we don't mean that the fire went out because He was there. No, it still burned. It was just that the burning wasn't worthy to be compared to the brilliancy of His presence. We never saw Him again. He only showed up when we needed Him most. But one thing was sure: We were glad they drug us from the presence of the wicked one into the presence of the Righteous One! In His presence we learned that, 'No weapon that is formed against thee shall prosper!'" (See Daniel 3.)

And if any man think that he knoweth any thing,
he knoweth nothing yet as he ought to know. But if
any man love God, the same is known of Him.

1 Corinthians 8:2-3

You need new meditations to dwell in your heart by faith, for your life will ultimately take on the direction of your thinking.

Many weaknesses, such as procrastination and laziness, are just draperies that cover up poor self-esteem and a lack of motivation. They are often symptoms of the subconscious avoiding the risk of failure.

God creates by speaking, but He speaks out of His own thoughts. Since God's Word says *"out of the abundance of the heart the mouth speaketh"* (Matt. 12:34b), then we go beyond the mouth to bring correction to the words we speak. We have to begin with the thoughts we think.

I pray that somehow the Spirit will reveal where you need Him to heal your thinking so you can possess what God wants you to have. Then you will be able to fully enjoy what He has given you. Many people have the blessing and still don't enjoy it because they conquered every foe except the enemy within!

Thou wilt show me the path of life: in Thy presence is fullness of joy; at Thy right hand there are pleasures for evermore.

Psalm 16:11

Have you begun your search for a closer manifestation of His grace? Your search alone is worship. When you seek Him, it suggests that you value Him and recognize His ability. The staggering, faulty steps of a seeker are far better than the stance of the complacent. He is not far away. He is in the furnace, moving in the ashes. Look closer. He is never far from the seeker who is on a quest to be in His presence.

Job said that God works on the left hand! The right hand in the Bible symbolizes power and authority. That's why Christ is seated on the right side of God (see Mark 16:19). "Right hand" means power. If you were to search for God, you would look on the right hand. Granted, He is on the right hand. He is full of authority, but His strength is made perfect in weakness (see 2 Cor. 12:9). He displays His glory in the ashes of human frailty. He works on the left hand!

For as many as are led by the Spirit of God, they are the sons of God. For ye have not received the spirit of bondage again to fear; but ye have received the Spirit of adoption, whereby we cry, Abba, Father. The Spirit itself beareth witness with our spirit, that we are the children of God.

Romans 8:14-16

King David brought Mephibosheth, the crippled son of Jonathan, to the palace. Even after Mephibosheth had been raised from the deplorable condition he was in, he was still so oppressed in his mind that he described himself as a "dead dog" (see 2 Sam. 9:8). He was a king's kid, but he saw himself as a dead dog!

Perception is everything. Mephibosheth thought of himself as a dead dog, so he lay on the floor like one. You have been on the floor long enough! It is time for a resurrection, and it is going to start in your mind.

Just because you've been treated like a dog doesn't make you one! Get up off the floor and take a seat at the Master's table—you are worthy. By virtue of His invitation, enjoy and rest in Him!

I thank my God always on your behalf, for the grace of God which is given you by Jesus Christ.

1 Corinthians 1:4

And when Jesus saw her, He called her to Him, and said unto her, Woman, thou art loosed from thine infirmity. And He laid His hands on her: and immediately she was made straight, and glorified God. ...And when He had said these things, all His adversaries were ashamed: and all the people rejoiced for all the glorious things that were done by Him.

Luke 13:12-13,17

Praise is contagious. Although the Bible doesn't say so, I imagine that those who saw Jesus heal the infirm woman were caught up in praise as well. The Church also must join in praise when the broken are healed. Those who missed the great blessing that day were those who decided to argue about religion.

Christ unleashed power in the infirm woman that day. He healed her body and gave her the strength of character to keep a proper attitude. The woman who is broken today will find power unleashed within her too, when she responds to the call and brings her wounds to the Great Physician.

The Lord works out everything for His own ends—
even the wicked for a day of disaster.

Proverbs 16:4 NIV

Great growth doesn't come into your life through mountaintop experiences. Great growth comes through the valleys and low places where you feel limited and vulnerable. The time God is really moving in your life may seem to be the lowest moment you have ever experienced. God is working on you, your faith and your character, when the blessing is delayed. The blessing is the reward that comes after you learn obedience through the things you suffered while waiting for it!

The prerequisite of the mountain is the valley. If there is no valley, there is no mountain. After you've been through this process a few times, you begin to realize that the valley is only a sign that with a few more steps, you'll be at the mountain again! So just hold on!

If you've been through a period that didn't seem to have the slightest stirring and God seems to stay still, the answer is no! God hasn't forgotten. Sometimes He moves openly. But sometimes He moves silently, working in the shadows. You can't see Him, but He is working!

But the Lord is faithful, who shall stablish you, and keep you from evil. And we have confidence in the Lord touching you, that ye both do and will do the things which we command you.

2 Thessalonians 3:3-4

Your confession is great. You've fought and defended yourself against attackers, and you have seen some increase; but when you allow God to heal your thoughts, you will explode into another dimension. Sometimes we have been strong because we had great struggles. We fought valiantly in the face of the enemies of life. However, when sunset falls on the battlefield, and after the troops have gone home, we hang up our gear and wish we were as valiant inwardly as we displayed outwardly!

Perceive and believe what God is doing in you. If you can get that in your head, you can reap it in your life! The harvest field that God wants to plant is in your head. Amidst all your troubles, hold onto your field of dreams. If you can water your own field when men are trying to command a drought in your life, God will mightily sustain you.

Behold, happy is the man whom God correcteth: therefore despise not thou the chastening of the Almighty: for He maketh sore, and bindeth up: He woundeth, and His hands make whole. He shall deliver thee in six troubles: yea, in seven there shall no evil touch thee.

Job 5:17-19

Listen for God's hammering in the spirit. It appears that He is not there, but He is.

Perhaps you've said, "Where is the move of God that I used to experience? Why am I going through these fiery trials?" God is there with you even now. He is operating in a different realm.

I know so well how hard it is to trust Him when you can't trace Him! But that's exactly what He wants you to do—He wants you to trust Him with either hand. It may seem that everybody is passing you right now. Avoid measuring yourself against other people. God knows when the time is right. His methods may seem crude and His teachings laborious, but His results will be simply breathtaking. Without scams and games, without trickery or politics, God will accomplish a supernatural miracle because you trusted Him while He worked in the invisible realm.

*Now he that ministereth seed to the sower both
minister bread for your food, and multiply your
seed sown, and increase the fruits of your righteousness.*

2 Corinthians 9:10b

I pray that this word is so powerful and personal, so intimate and applicable, that it leaves behind it a barren
mind made pregnant. This seed of greatness will explode
in your life and harvest in your children, feeding the generations to come and changing the winds of destiny.

As we move on to other issues and face our inner selves,
we strip away our facades and see ourselves as we really
are. We need to not be fearful of our nakedness nor discouraged by our flaws.

In my heart I smell an approaching rain. Moisture is in
the air and the clouds have gathered. Our fields have
been chosen for the next rain and the wind started to
blow. Run into the field with your precious seeds and
plant them in the soft ground of your fertile mind. Whatever you plant in the evening will be reaped in the morning. I am so excited for you. I just heard a clap of
thunder…in just another moment, there'll be rain!

But we all, with open face beholding as in a glass the glory of the Lord, are changed into the same image from glory to glory, even as by the Spirit of the Lord.

2 Corinthians 3:18

Soon you will be reshaped and remade into a gold chalice from which only the King can drink. All dross is discarded; all fear is removed. Spectators will ask how such a wonderful vessel was made out of such poor materials. They will behold the jewels of your testimony and the brilliant glory of that fresh anointing. Some will wonder if you are the same person that they used to know.

Now you sit on the Master's right side, ready and available to be used, a vessel of honor unto Him. No matter how glorious it is to sit on His right hand and be brought to a position of power, remember that you were once boiled down and hollowed out. Look back over your life. Taste the bitter tears and the cold winds of human indifference and never let anyone make you forget. You've not always been where you are. What can I say? You've come a long way, baby!

Jesus did many other miraculous signs in the presence of His disciples, which are not recorded in this book. But these are written that you may believe that Jesus is the Christ, the Son of God, and that by believing you may have life in His name.

John 20:30-31 NIV

The best parts of school when I was an 8-year-old boy were recess and the walk home from school. The walk home would lead down Troy Road toward "old man Harless' " store. A quarter of mine was saved for the brightly colored books that were stacked in a display for all the children to see…Superman and Captain Marvel, Captain America and Spiderman. I would purchase a copy of the latest issue and imagine that I was one of these men, a super hero who could transform as needed into anything necessary to destroy the villain.

We believed in possibility, and though we were neither wealthy nor affluent, we could escape like a bird through the window of a full-color magazine and become anybody we wanted to be for at least 30 minutes—before my mother's voice would be heard from the rickety back porch behind the house.

But I would have you without carefulness. He that is unmarried careth for the things that belong to the Lord, how he may please the Lord, how he may please the Lord: but he that is married careth for the things that are of the world, how he may please his wife....

1 Corinthians 7:32-34

Some of you do not understand the benefits of being single. In reality, while you're not married, you really ought to be involved with God. When you get married, you direct all of the training that you had while you were unmarried toward your spouse.

Single women often forget some very important advantages they have. You can pray whenever and however you please. You can lie prostrate on the floor in your house and worship and no one will become annoyed about it.

Often those who minister in churches hear unmarried women complain about their need for a husband, but rarely does a single woman boast about the kind of relationship she is free to build with the Lord. While a woman is single she has the unique opportunity to build herself up in the Lord without the drains that can occur later.

And what shall I more say? for time would fail me to tell of Gedeon, and of Barak, and of Samson, and of Jephthae; of David also, and Samuel, and of the prophets: who through faith subdued kingdoms, wrought righteousness, obtained promises, stopped the mouths of lions, quenched the violence of fire, escaped the edge of the sword....

Hebrews 11:32-34

We need heroes today. We need someone who has accomplished something to give us the courage to believe in the invisible and feel the intangible. We need role models and men whose shadows we may stand in, men who provide a cool refreshing place of safety away from the despair of our oppressive society. It's just that all the "supermen" in the Church seem to have somehow gotten zapped by "kryptonite." Either they or their reputations have wilted into the abyss of human failure.

What are we going to do as we face this generation? From drug-using political officials to prostitute-purchasing preachers, the stars are falling on the heads of this generation! All of their wonder and dreams have turned into a comic book—a comic book that somehow doesn't seem funny anymore. Where did the heroes go?

*Whom have I in heaven but Thee? And there is
none upon the earth that I desire beside Thee.*

Psalm 73:25

The Lord wants to make sweet love to you. I'm not
being carnal, I'm being real. He wants to hold you.
He wants you to come in at the end of the day and say,
"Oh, Lord, I could hardly make it today. Whew, I went
through so much today. I'm so glad I have You in my life.
They tried to devour me, but I thank You for this time we
have together. I just couldn't wait to get alone and worship You and praise You and magnify You. You're the One
who keeps me going. You're the lover of my soul, my
mind, my emotions, my attitude and my disposition.
Hold me. Touch me, strengthen me. Let me hold You. Let
me bless You. I've set the night aside for us. I'm not so
busy that I don't have time for You. If I have no time for
You, I have no time for anyone. I am holy in body and in
spirit. I am not committing adultery in our relationship.
My body is Yours."

If we say that we have no sin, we deceive ourselves, and the truth is not in us. If we confess our sins, He is faithful and just to forgive our sins, and to cleanse us from all unrighteousness.

John 1:8-9

O ur healing will require more than a processional of religious ideas that are neither potent nor relevant. We need to understand that God is able to repair the broken places, but it requires us to expose where those broken places are. If we don't say to Him, "This is where I am hurting," then how can He pour in the oil and the wine?

We need to lay ourselves before Him and seek His face in the beauty of holiness—the holiness that produces wholeness. It is in these moments that we are forced to reevaluate our concepts. Have we misaligned ourselves with God, or were our goals "out of kilter" to begin with? This isn't a matter of one denomination arguing with another over who is right; it is a matter of a broken family seeking healing and answers that can only come from the presence of God. I am convinced He can heal whatever we can confess!

*One thing have I desired of the Lord, that will I seek
after; that I may dwell in the house of the Lord all
the days of my life, to behold the beauty of the Lord,
and to inquire in His temple.*

Psalm 27:4

There is nothing wrong with wanting to be married.
Simply take care of the Lord while you're waiting.
Minister to Him. Let Him heal you, and worship Him.
Single women ought to be the most consecrated women
in the Church. Instead of singles being envious of married women, the married ought to be jealous of singles.
You are in a position and posture of prayer. The Lord has
become your necessary food. While some married
women are dependent on their husbands, single women
learn to be dependent on the Lord. God has no limitations. A married woman may have a husband who can do
some things, but God can do everything. What a privilege to be married to Him. He told Joel, *"And upon the
handmaids...will I pour out My spirit"* (Joel 2:29). God
has a special anointing for the woman who is free to seek
Him. Her prayer life should explode in miracles!

I exhort therefore, that, first of all, supplications, prayers, intercessions, and giving of thanks, be made for all men; for kings, for all that are in authority; that we may lead a quiet and peaceable life in all godliness and honesty.

1 Timothy 2:1-2 [Ref. 1 John 1:8-9]

God knew who we were when He called us. Perhaps the sharp contrast between the people God uses and the God who uses them is to provide the worshiper with a clear distinction of who is to be worshiped!

It is undeniable that we face faltering visions and visionaries. Let us seek God for His divine purpose. Could it possibly be that God's intent is to establish believable heroes?

We need no glaring, high-polished people for this day! We need heroes whose tarnished suits cannot hide their open hearts or their need to touch broken lives. The cry is going out for something believable—for something that even if not glorious, is at least fathomable.

The stress of trying to impress others with presentations of spiraling spiritual altitudes has produced isolation and intimidation. No wonder our leaders are dying in the pulpit and suffering from an epidemic of heart attacks and strokes!

Brethren, I count not myself to have apprehended:
but this one thing I do, forgetting those things
which are behind, and reaching forth unto those
things which are before, I press toward the mark for
the prize of the high calling of God in Christ Jesus.

Philippians 3:13-14

Alas, the call is a high calling. Yet it has been answered by lowly men who had the discernment to see a God high and lifted up. They stood on their toes like children, but still fell short of reaching His splendor. In short, the heroes in the Bible were not perfect, but they were powerful! They were not superhuman, but they were revelatory. Often chastised and corrected, they were still not discarded, for the Lord was with them.

Jesus was forever having to correct His disciples. Their pettiness, their anger and stinginess—these faults often reaffirmed the fact that they were "men of like passions." I, for one, am glad that they were. Their human frailties encourage the rest of us that we too can be used by God in spite of our feeble, crippled, and fragmented attempts at piety and true devotion.

I beseech you therefore, brethren, by the mercies of God, that ye present your bodies a living sacrifice, holy, acceptable unto God, which is your reasonable service.

Romans 12:1

Being single and devoted to God does not mean it is wrong for you to want physical companionship. God ordained that need. While you are waiting, though, understand that God thinks He's your husband. Be careful how you treat Him. He thinks He's your man. That's why He does those special favors for you. It is God who made you into a beautiful woman. He has been taking care of you, even when you didn't notice His provision. He is the source of every good thing. He provides for your daily care. It is He who opened doors for you. He has been your friend and your companion.

Maybe you haven't been living like you really should. Maybe your house hasn't been the house of prayer that it really could have been. I want you to take this opportunity and begin to sanctify your house and body. Maybe your body has been mauled and pawed by all sorts of people. Give your body as a living sacrifice to God.

"For I know the plans I have for you," declares the Lord, "plans to prosper you and not to harm you, plans to give you a hope and a future.

Jeremiah 29:11 NIV

Let's not glamorize sin. Sin is sin and it stinks in the nostrils of God. But have our noses become more sensitive than God's? Would we, like the others outside the tomb, choose to condemn to an eternal grave the man Lazarus, whose decomposing body had been shut up in a tomb for three days and begun to stink? Thank God that Jesus didn't let the stink stop Him from saving the man.

You have to be a hero to even expose yourself to the jealousy and cruelty of being raised up as a leader. They often receive blows from satan and stabs from friends.

It is imperative that our vision be both progressive and regressive. In the forefront of our minds must be a plan that promises bright hopes for the future. There must be a strong sense of destiny lodged firmly in our minds that dispels the despair of past failures. We must live our lives facing the rising sun.

Let the husband render unto the wife due benevolence: and likewise also the wife unto the husband.

1 Corinthians 7:3

When God picks a wife for one of His royal sons, He will pick her from those who are faithful and holy unto Him. He may pass over those who didn't keep a vow to Him. If you will marry a king, he will have claimed you to be a queen. Begin to sanctify yourself. Bring your body before God. Bring your nature before God. Bring your passion to Him. Allow God to plug into your need.

Allow God to strengthen you. From the crown of my head to the soles of my feet, all that I am belongs to God. Early in the morning will I seek His face. I lie upon my bed at night and call on His name. I'll touch Him, embrace Him. He is the God of my salvation."

Marriage is ministry. If you are single, your ministry is directly unto the Lord. If you are married, your ministry is through your spouse. Then you learn how to be devoted to God through the relationship you have with your spouse.

Brethren, I count not myself to have apprehended:
but this one thing I do, forgetting those things
which are behind, and reaching forth unto those
things which are before, I press toward the mark for
the prize of the high calling of God in Christ Jesus.

Philippians 3:13-14

Although heroes don't have to be perfect, they must be resilient enough to survive tragedy and adversity. All of us have experienced the pain of adversity in our warfare, whether it was physical, emotional, economical, spiritual, or sexual. Regardless of where the attack falls, they are very personal in nature. Real heroes not only survive the incident, but overcome the lingering effects that often come from it.

The people referred to in Hebrews 11 were not mindful of where they came from. Their minds were full of where they were going. Whatever your mind is full of, that is where you eventually move.

If you don't survive, you can't save anyone. No young man in a combat zone can carry his wounded comrade if he himself does not survive. Live long enough to invest the wealth of your experience in the release of some other victim whom satan desires to incapacitate!

Strengthened with all might, according to His glorious power, unto all patience and longsuffering with joyfulness.

Colossians 1:11

———

The Scriptures declare that its heroes were made strong out of weakness. In order to be a real success, you must be able to be strengthened through struggle. What we need is a hero who can, as these men did, report back to the world that he escaped. He may have felt weak, he may have cried and suffered, but he still made it.

Look at these men mentioned in Hebrews 11:32. Examine their lives. They were not glaring examples of flawless character; yet they epitomized faith toward God. Even though most of them experienced failures and flaws, they would have made the front pages of the newspapers in our day for their heroism. We must be careful when judging the weak moments in their lives. Consider the entirety of their lives and you will see that the dent in their armor didn't affect their performance on the battlefield.

Gideon failed the biblical faith test when he sought a sign. Samson shined on the battlefield but had struggles in the bedroom. They still made it to the list of faith.

Behold, I stand at the door, and knock: if any man hear My voice, and open the door, I will come in to him, and will sup with him, and he with Me.

Revelation 3:20

Marriage is the place in human society where true love can be expressed in a great way. Marriage partners are to give self-sacrificially to one another. Jesus gave Himself for the Church. So also do husbands and wives give themselves to each other. Marriage is not a place where we seek self-gratification. It is the place where we seek to gratify another.

The sacredness of marriage is found in the relationship between Christ and the Church. Jesus continues to intercede on behalf of the Church, even after He gave His all for us. He is the greatest advocate of believers. He stands before God to defend and proclaim our value. Similarly, husbands and wives are to be bonded together to the extent that they become the greatest advocate of the other. Not demanding one's own way, but always seeking to please the other.

There can be no doubt that God has special plans for each one of us. Enjoy being a whole person.

He is despised and rejected of men; a man of sorrows, and acquainted with grief: and we hid as it were our faces from Him; He was despised and we esteemed Him not.

Isaiah 53:3

When we have been ostracized by someone or something that we wanted to belong to, our streaming tears cannot soften the hard truth. Rejection tastes like bile in our gut. However, the experience can make us bitter, or it can make us better. I choose better. What about you?

I believe this kind of pain causes us to achieve a level of consecration that is out of the reach of people who have never been rejected. Once the reality hits us that God purposely chooses to use misplaced and rejected people, then first and foremost, we experience a sense of gratitude that flows through our human hearts like hot syrup. It fills every crack and crevice of our minds, which suggested there was no place of meaning for us. It is in the shadows of these moments that we worship, enveloped in the love of the sacrificed Lamb of God, the God who created a place for the misplaced and chose us for Himself.

...and things which are despised, hath God chosen, yea, and things which are not , to bring to nought things that are: That no flesh should glory in His presence....

1 Corinthians 1:29-31

I must confess that more than once I have seen His hand pick up the pieces of this broken heart and restore back to service my crushed emotions and murky confidence, while I stood in awe at the fact that God can do so much with so little.

The greatest place to preach isn't in our great meetings with swelling crowds and lofty recognitions. The greatest place to preach is in the trenches, in the foxholes and the hog pens of life. If you want a grateful audience, take your message to the messy places of life and scrape the hog hairs off the prodigal sons of God who were locked away in the hog pens by the spiritual elite.

It is time for us to redefine and redirect our gaze to find the heroes of God among us. We must not forget that God purposely chooses to use misplaced and rejected people, and He may be looking in our direction.

And the Lord God caused a deep sleep to fall upon Adam, and he slept: and He took one of his ribs, and closed up the flesh instead thereof; and the rib, which the Lord God had taken from man, made He a woman, and brought her unto the man.

Genesis 2:21-22

The woman was made, fashioned out of the man, to be a help meet. Through their union, they find wholeness in each other. She helps him meet and accomplish his task. If you have a power saw, it has great potential for cutting. However, it is ineffective until it is plugged in. The receptacle helps the power saw meet its purpose. Without that receptacle, the power saw, although mighty, remains limited.

However, there is a vulnerability about the receptacle. They must be careful what kind of plug they are connected with. Receptacles are open. Women are open by nature and design. Men are closed. You must be careful what you allow to plug into you and draw strength from you. The wrong plugs may drain your power.

God recognizes your vulnerability. His design included the commitment of a covenant. Nothing short of this commitment meets His standard.

And God said, Let Us make man in Our image,
after Our likeness: and let them have dominion over
the fish of the sea, and over the fowl of the air, and
over the cattle, and over all the earth, and over
every creeping thing that creepeth upon the earth.

Genesis 1:26

Originally, God created humanity perfect and good. In Genesis chapter 3, we see that Eve allowed herself to be taken advantage of by satan, who plugged into her desire to see, taste, and be wise. *"And the man said, The woman whom Thou gavest to be with me, she gave me of the tree, and I did eat"* (Gen. 3:12).

Eve had given her attention over to someone else. *"And the Lord God said unto the woman, What is this that thou hast done? And the woman said, The serpent beguiled me, and I did eat"* (Gen. 3:13). Adam's anger is shown by his statement, "You gave her to be with me." The woman answered, "Well, I couldn't help it. He plugged into me, or he beguiled me."

You've got to be careful who you let uncover you, because they can lead you to complete destruction.

> *Wherefore seeing we also are compassed about with so great a cloud of witnesses, let us lay aside every weight, and the sin which doth so easily beset us, and let us run with patience the race that is set before us.*
>
> *Hebrews 12:1*

A runner trains himself to achieve a goal. That goal ultimately is to break the ribbon, the mark of success. If there is no prize beyond the goal, then the race seems in vain. No runner would run a race and then receive the broken ribbon as the symbol of his success. At the end of the race is a prize unrelated to the race itself—a trophy that can be given only to people who have reached the pinnacle of accomplishment. What we must understand as we ascend toward God's purpose is it blesses God when we attain what we were created to attain. It is His eternal purpose that we pursue. However, we can be blessed only by the God behind the purpose. If we build a great cathedral for the Lord and fail to touch the God whom the cathedral is for, what good is the building aside from God?

The weapons we fight with are not the weapons of the world. On the contrary, they have divine power to demolish strongholds.

2 Corinthians 10:4 NIV

In Genesis chapter 3, we see that Eve allowed herself to be taken advantage of by satan, who plugged into her desire to see, taste, and be wise. The enemy took advantage of her weakness.

He is attracted to you because he knows that you were designed as a receptacle to help meet someone's vision. If he can get you to help meet his vision, you will have great problems. God said, *"And I will put enmity between thee and the woman, and between thy seed and her seed"* (Gen. 3:15a).

There is a special conflict between the woman and the enemy. You must do spiritual warfare against the enemy because you are vulnerable in certain areas and there is enmity between you and the enemy. You must be on your guard. Women tend to be more prayerful than men, once they are committed. If you are a woman living today and you're not learning spiritual warfare, you're in trouble. The enemy may be taking advantage of you.

But I fear, lest by any means, as the serpent beguiled Eve through his subtlety, so your minds should be corrupted from the simplicity that is in Christ.

2 Corinthians 11:3

There is a fight between you and the devil. Over and over again, satan is attacking and assaulting your femininity.

Mass populations of women have increased over the country. The Bible says that the time will come when there will be seven women to every one man (see Isa. 4:1). Statistics indicate that we are living in those times right now. Where you have more need than supply, there is growing enmity between the woman and the enemy. Satan is continually attacking femininity.

If godly women do not learn how to start praying and doing effective spiritual warfare, they will not discern what is plugging into them. Perhaps you become completely vulnerable to moods and attitudes and dispositions. Perhaps you are doing things and you don't know why. Something's plugging into you. If you are tempted to rationalize, "I'm just in a bad mood. I don't know just what it is. I'm just evil. I'm tough," don't believe it. Something's plugging into you.

But if someone obeys God's teaching, then in that person God's love has truly reached its goal.

1 John 2:5 NCV

As an eagle stirs her nest, so God must challenge us to leave the familiar places and perform the uncertain future of putting into practice the total of all we have learned in the Lord's presence. As Isaiah said, *"Here am I; send me"* (Isa. 6:8), go from the gluttony of storing up the treasure to being a vessel God can use!

The other extreme is equally, if not more, dangerous. What makes us think we can do the work of the Lord and never spend time with the Lord of the work? We get burned out when we do not keep fresh fire burning within! We need the kind of fire that comes from putting down all the work and saying to the Lord, "I need my time with You." What good is it to break the finish line if you do not go beyond that temporary moment of self-aggrandizement to receive a valued reward? The accomplishment isn't reward enough because once it is attained, it ceases to be alluring.

And Adam called his wife's name Eve; because she was the mother of all living.

Genesis 3:20

In Genesis 3:16, God explained that birthing comes through sorrow. Everything you bring forth comes through pain. If it didn't come through pain, it probably wasn't worth much. If you're going to bring forth—and I'm not merely talking about babies, I'm talking about birthing vision and purpose—you will do so with sorrow and pain. If you're going to bring forth anything in your career, your marriage or your life, if you're going to develop anything in your character, if you're going to be a fruitful woman, it's going to come through sorrow. It will come through the things you suffer. You will enter into strength through sorrow.

Sorrow is not the object; it's simply the canal that the object comes through. Many mistake sorrow for the baby instead of the canal. In that case, all you have is pain. For every sorrow, you ought to have something to show for it. Don't let the devil give you sorrow without seed. Any time you have sorrow, it is a sign that God is trying to get something through you and to you.

But we were gentle among you, even as a nurse cherisheth her children: so being affectionately desirous of you, we were willing to have imparted unto you, not the gospel of God only, but also our own souls, because ye were dear unto us.

1 Thessalonians 2:7-8

When you see sorrow multiply, it is a sign that God is getting ready to send something to you. Don't settle for the pain and not get the benefit. Hold out. Disregard the pain and get the promise. Understand that God has promised some things to you that He wants you to have, and you've got to stay there on the table until you get to the place where you ought to be in the Lord. After all, the pain is forgotten when the baby is born.

What is the pain when compared with the baby? Some may have dropped the baby. That happens when you become so engrossed with the pain that you leave the reward behind you. Your attention gets focused on the wrong thing. You can be so preoccupied with how bad it hurts that you miss the joy of a vision giving birth.

If any man's work abide which he hath built there-upon, he shall receive a reward.

1 Corinthians 3:14

Release comes so you can enter the presence of God to be restored. To be restored means to be built back up, to be restocked. Only God can put back into you what striving took out. You need to strive, but you don't need the obsession that it can create. There will never be anything that God gives you to do that will replace what God's mere presence will give. You will never build your self-esteem by accomplishing goals because, as in the case of my twins, once you've done it, it's done! No lasting affirmation comes from a mountain that has been climbed.

Only Christ can save you, affirm you, and speak to how you feel about yourself. The praises of men will fall into the abyss of a leaky heart. When you have a crack, everything in you will leak out. Let God fix it. Your job can't do it. Sex can't do it. Marriage can't do it. Another graduate degree can't do it, but God can! He is the Doctor who specialized in reconstructive surgery!

No discipline seems pleasant at the time, but painful. Later on, however, it produces a harvest of righteousness and peace for those who have been trained by it.

Hebrews 12:11 NIV

For every struggle in your life, God accomplished something in your character and in your spirit. Why hold the pain and drop the baby when you could hold the baby and drop the pain? You are holding on to the wrong thing if all you do is concentrate on past pain. Release the pain. Pain doesn't fall off on its own. It's got to be released. Allow God to loose you from the pain, separate you from what has afflicted you and be left with the baby and not the problem.

He said, *"In sorrow thou shalt bring forth children"* (Gen. 3:16b). That includes every area of your life. That's in your character. It is true in your spirit as well as in your finances. If it comes into this world, it has to come through you. If you're in a financial rut, bring forth. If you're in need of healing for your body, bring forth. Understand that it must be brought forth. It doesn't just happen by accident.

Beareth all things, believeth all things, hopeth all things, endureth all things.

1 Corinthians 13:7

G od will not allow you to become trapped in a situa-tion without escape. But you've got to push while you are in pain if you intend to produce.

There remains a conflict between past pain and future desire. Here is the conflict. He said, *"...in sorrow thou shalt bring forth children; and thy desire shall be to thy husband, and he shall rule over thee"* (Gen. 3:16). In other words, you have so much pain in producing the child that, if you don't have balance between past pain and future desire, you will quit producing. God says, "After the pain, your desire shall be to your husband." Pain is swallowed by desire.

Impregnated with destiny, women of promise must bear down in the spirit. The past hurts; the pain is genuine. However, you must learn to get in touch with something other than your pain. If you do not have desire, you won't have the tenacity to resurrect. Desire will come back. After the pain is over, desire follows, because it takes desire to be productive again.

The four and twenty elders fall down before Him that sat on the throne, and worship Him that liveth for ever and ever, and cast their crowns before the throne, saying, Thou art worthy, O Lord, to receive glory and honor and power; for Thou hast created all things, and for Thy pleasure they are and were created.

Revelation 4:10-11

There is a place in the presence of God where crowns lose their luster. There is a place where the accolades of men sound brash and out of pitch. There is a place where all our memorials of great accomplishments seem like dusty stones gathered by bored children who had nothing better to collect. There are times when we trade success for solace. In Revelation, 24 elders traded their golden, jewel-encrusted crowns for a tear-stained moment in the presence of a blood-stained Lamb. Many wonderful people are suffering with their success because they cannot discern when to throw down their crowns and just worship.

Many people don't learn about themselves and the things they hold on to. They need to learn when to let go! Just throw your crown down at the throne of God!

There is surely a future hope for you, and your hope will not be cut off.

Proverbs 23:18 NIV

Until the desire to go forward becomes greater than the memories of past pain, you will never hold the power to create again. However, when the desire comes back into your spirit and begins to live in you again, it will release you from the pain.

God wants to give us the strength to overcome past pain and move forward into new life. Solomon wrote, *"Where there is no vision, the people perish"* (Prov. 29:18a). Vision is the desire to go ahead. Until you have a vision to go ahead, you will always live in yesterday's struggles. The devil wants you to live in yesterday. He's always telling you about what you cannot do. His method is to bring up your past. He wants to draw your attention backward.

God wants to put desire in the spirit of broken women. There wouldn't be any desire if there wasn't any relationship. You can't desire something that's not there. The very fact that you have a desire is in itself an indication that better days are coming. Expect something wonderful to happen.

Because the creature itself also shall be delivered from the bondage of corruption into the glorious liberty of the children of God.

Romans 8:12

———•—•———

When I was a boy, we had a dog named Pup. He was a mean and ferocious animal. We had him chained in the back of the house to a four-by-four post. The chain was huge. We never imagined that he could possibly tear himself loose from that post. He would chase something and the chain would snap him back.

One day Pup saw something that he really wanted. It was out of his reach. He pulled that chain to the limit. All at once, instead of drawing him back, the chain snapped, and Pup was loose.

That's what God will do for you. The thing that used to pull you back you will snap, and you will be liberated by a goal because God's put greatness before you. You can't receive what God wants for your life by looking back. He is mighty. He is powerful enough to destroy the yoke of the enemy in your life. He is strong enough to bring you out and loose you, deliver you, and set you free.

And every creature which is in heaven, and on the earth, and under the earth, and such as are in the sea, and all that are in them, heard I saying, Blessing, and honor, and glory, and power, be unto Him that sitteth upon the throne, and unto the Lamb for ever and eve. And the four beats said, Amen. And the four and twenty elders fell down and worshipped Him the liveth for ever and ever.

Revelation 5:13-14

When you come into the presence of God cast down your crowns and bend your knees. You can let it go and still not lose it. Like the 24 elders in Revelation who threw their crowns before the throne, you must learn to trade a monument for a moment. The real reward can be paid only by the one who hired you—God Himself. You see, the 24 elders knew that they had received results and rewards, but the real credit went to the Lord. They were wise enough not to be too impressed with their own success. They knew that it was God all the time. When you give the glory to God, you will be fulfilled in His presence!

My substance was not hid from Thee, when I was made in secret, and curiously wrought in the lowest part of the earth.

Psalm 139:15

Put the truth in your spirit, and feed, nurture, and allow it to grow. Quit telling yourself you're too fat or old or ignorant. It is unwise to speak against your own body. Women tend to speak against their bodies, opening the door for sickness and disease. Speak life to your own body. Celebrate who you are. You are the image of God.

Scriptures remind us of who we are. *"I will praise Thee; for I am fearfully and wonderfully made: marvellous are Thy works; and that my soul knoweth right well"* (Ps. 139:14). These are the words that will feed our souls. The truth will allow new life to swell up within us. Feed the embryo within with such words as these.

"And the Lord shall make thee the head, and not the tail; and thou shalt be above only, and thou shalt not be beneath" (Deut. 28:13a). "I can do all things through Christ which strengtheneth me" (Phil. 4:13). The Word of God will provide the nourishment that will feed the baby inside.

Now faith is being sure of what we hope for and certain of what we do not see. This is what the ancients were commended for. By faith we understand that the universe was formed at God's command, so that what is seen was not made out of what was invisible.

Hebrews 11:1-3 NIV

We believe God, we are counted as righteous. Righteousness cannot be earned or merited. It comes only through faith. We can have a good report simply on the basis of our faith. Faith becomes the tender, like money is the legal tender in this world that we use for exchange of goods and services. Faith becomes the substance, of things hoped for, and the evidence of things not seen.

God wants us to understand that just because we can't see it, doesn't mean that He won't do it. God's purpose begins as a word that gets in the spirit. Everything that is tangible started as an intangible. It was a thought, a Word of God. In the same way, what man has invented began as a concept in someone's mind. So just because we don't see it, doesn't mean we won't get it.

Henceforth there is laid up for me a crown of right-eousness, which the Lord, the righteous judge, shall give me at that day: and not to me only, but unto all them also that love His appearing.

2 Timothy 4:8

Balance helps to keep you from falling. It does not guarantee that you won't fall, but it does safeguard against the possibility. Never lose your balance—it will assist you in being a person and not just a personality. Ordinary people who have extraordinary callings are the order of the day in this age. You will see in this age God raising Davids to the forefront, not Sauls. He will raise up men who don't look as if they would be kings. When you get your crown, don't use it to belittle people who need you. Instead cast it at the feet of the Lord who is the Giver of gifts as well as the preferred Prize of all that He gives.

Prayer is the helm that turns the ship toward the winds of destiny. Steal away and fill your arms with the presence of your Father embracing you so you can affect people.

*He hath made every thing beautiful in His time:
also He hath set the world in their heart, so that no
man can find out the work that God maketh from
the beginning to the end.*

Ecclesiastes 3:11

The writer of Hebrews mentions many areas of Abraham's faith. Abraham looked for a city whose "builder and maker" was God (Heb. 11:10). If Abraham was famous for anything, it should have been for producing Isaac. However, he is not listed in the faith "hall of fame" as the one who produced Isaac.

"Through faith also Sarah herself received strength to conceive seed, and was delivered of a child when she was past age, because she judged Him faithful who had promised" (Heb. 11:11). When it comes to bringing forth the baby, the Scriptures do not refer to a man; they refer to a womb-man.

Sarah needed strength to conceive seed when she was past childbearing age. God met her need. She believed that He was capable of giving her a child regardless of what the circumstances looked like. From a natural perspective, it was impossible. The enemy certainly didn't want it to happen. God, however, performed His promise.

Lord, Thou hast heard the desire of the humble:
Thou wilt prepare their heart, Thou wilt cause
Thine ear to hear.

Psalm 10:17

Why would you allow your vision to be incapacitated for the lack of a man? Many women have unbelieving husbands at home. Have faith for yourself. Be a womb-man. It doesn't matter whether someone else believes or not; you cling to the truth that He is doing a good work in you.

You are God's woman. You are not called to sit by the window waiting on God to send you a husband. You had better have some faith yourself and believe God down in your own spirit. If you would believe God, He would perform His Word in your life. No matter the desire or the blessing that you seek, God has promised to give you the desires of your heart.

Recognize that where life has seemed irrational and out of control, He will turn it around. When trouble was breaking loose in my life, and I thought I couldn't take it anymore, God intervened and broke every chain that held me back. He will do no less for you.

After this manner therefore pray ye: Our Father which art in heaven, hallowed be Thy name.

Matthew 6:9

———————

When Jesus taught on prayer, He was teaching us how to steer the ship of life through the boisterous winds of adversity. If we can follow the "manner" of prayer, then we can follow the course of life. In order to pray effectively, we must know the personage of God. Hence He said, *"Our Father."* This establishes the basis of the relationship that we have with God. He is more than just Creator—He is our Father.

"Which art in heaven" addresses the fact that the God I am related to is the Ruler of the universe. He sits on the circle of the earth. The Bible teaches us that Heaven is God's throne. So when we say, "which art in heaven," we are proclaiming the absolute sovereignty of our Father.

"I am not ashamed to praise You as I know the extent of Your authority. I take this time to approach You correctly. *'Hallowed be Thy name.'*" Praise will turn God's head. It will get His attention. When you praise His name, you are praising His character. He is holy!

And they that be wise shall shine as the brightness of the firmament; and they that turn many to righteousness as the stars for ever and ever.

Daniel 12:3

Abraham had many promises from God regarding his descendants. God told Abraham that his seed would be as the sands of the sea and the stars of Heaven.

There were two promises of seed given to Abraham. God said his seed would be as the sands of the earth. That promise represents the natural, physical nation of Israel. These were the people of the Old Covenant. However, God didn't stop there. He also promised that Abraham's seed would be as the stars of Heaven. These are the people of the New Covenant, the exalted people. That's the Church. We are exalted in Christ Jesus. We too are seed of Abraham. We are the stars of Heaven.

God planned a new spiritual Kingdom that will last forever. The plan started as a seed, but it ended up as stars.

Whatever God gives you, He wants it to be multiplied in the womb of your spirit. When you bring it forth, it shall be greater than the former.

Thy kingdom come. Thy will be done in earth, as it is in heaven. Give us this day our daily bread. And forgive us our debts, as we forgive our debtors.

Matthew 6:1-12

"Thy kingdom come" releases the downpour of the power of God. Praise will cause the very power of God to come down in your life. But what good is power without purpose? Jesus taught, *"Thy will be done in earth, as it is in heaven."* That is a step up from power to purpose. Now the purpose of God comes down to your life. You can't have success without purpose!

"Give us this day our daily bread" deals with the provisions of Heaven coming down. This is more than a prayer; it is a divine direction. After receiving power in your life, you come to understand the purpose. If you know your purpose, God will release the provisions.

"Forgive us our debts, as we forgive our debtors." There's nothing like provisions to give you the grace to forgive. It is easier to forgive when you discover that your enemies didn't stop the blessing from coming. Jesus teaches us to pray for the penitence of a forgiving heart.

Yea, though I walk through the valley of the shadow of death, I will fear no evil: for Thou art with me; Thy rod and Thy staff they comfort me.

Psalm 23:4

The enemy wants to multiply fear in your life. He wants you to become so afraid that you won't be able to figure out what you fear. You may be frightened to live in your own home. Some are afraid to correct their children. Some people fear standing up in front of others. God wants to set you free from fear as you are filled with faith.

In order to move forward, we must be willing to give up yesterday and go on toward tomorrow. We have to trust God enough to allow Him to come in and plow up our lives. Perhaps He needs to root out closet skeletons and replace them with new attitudes.

God deals directly with the issues of the heart and lets you know you do not have to be afraid. The plans of God are good. He is not like the people who have hurt and abused you. He wants only to help you be completely restored.

He that hath an ear, let him hear what the Spirit saith unto the churches.

Revelation 2:29

Every aspect of creation that receives anything, gives it back to God. The mineral kingdom gives strength to the vegetable kingdom. The vegetable kingdom is consumed by the animal kingdom. Everything reaches the point of return.

We as Christians reach fulfillment when we come to the point where we bring to the Lord all that we have and worship Him on the other side of accomplishment. There is a ringing in the heart of a believer that requires an answer. He is calling us through our triumphs and conquests. A deep sound in the recesses of a heart turned toward God suggests that there is a deeper relationship on the other side of the blessing. As wonderful as it is to be blessed with promises, there is still a faint ringing that suggests the Blesser is better than the blessing. It is a ringing that many people overlook. The noise of the bustling, blaring sound of survival can be deafening. There must be a degree of spirituality in order to hear and respond to the inner ringing of the call of God!

The Lord openeth the eyes of the blind: the Lord raiseth them that are bowed down: the Lord loveth the righteous.

Psalm 146:8

Maybe you have been tormented and in pain. You have been upset. You have been frustrated. It is hindering your walk. God is releasing you from fear. You need to allow Him an opportunity in your life. Then you will start seeing beauty at all different stages of your life. Maybe you have been afraid of aging. God will give you the strength to thank Him for every year. Celebrate who you have become through His assistance. In every circumstance, rejoice that He was with you in it.

I believe God is bringing health into dry bones, bones that were bowed over, bones that were bent out of shape, bones that made you upset with yourself. All are giving way to the life of the Spirit. Perhaps you responded to your history with low self-esteem. God will heal the inner wound and teach you how important you are to Him. You do make a difference. The world would be a different place if it were not for you. You are a part of His divine plan.

We are of God. He who knows God hears us; he who is not of God does not hear us.

1 John 4:6 NKJV

I can think of no better illustration of this concept than the ten lepers in the Bible (see Luke 17:11-19). These ten men were entombed by the prison of their own limitations. No matter who they were before, now they were lepers. They were separated and cast out from friends and family. Like all alienated groups, their only refuge was in each other's company. Ten men huddled together on the side of the road heard that Jesus was passing by. The most frightening thing that could happen in any hurting person's life is for Jesus to just pass by. These men, however, seized the moment. They took a risk…they cried out to Him. Desperate people do desperate things. Have you ever had a moment in your life that pushed you into a radical decision? These lepers cried out!

No one can hear like the Lord does. He can hear your thoughts afar off (see Ps. 139:2), so you know He can hear the desperate cry of someone who has nothing left to lose.

> *And such were some of you: but ye are washed,*
> *but ye are sanctified, but ye are justified in the*
> *name of the Lord Jesus, and by the Spirit of our*
> *God.*
>
> 1 Corinthians 6:11

If you have been wondering how God will make things come to pass in your life, remember that He will accomplish the task. No man will get the credit for your deliverance. The angel told Mary, *"The Holy Ghost shall come upon thee"* (Luke 1:35). I believe the same is true of godly women today. The Holy Spirit will fill you. He will impregnate you. He will give life to your spirit. He will put purpose back into you. He will renew you. He will restore you.

God had a special plan for Mary. She brought forth Jesus. He has a special plan for us. We, however, aren't privileged to see the future. We don't know what kind of good things He has in store for us. But, He has a plan. God's women are to be womb-men. They are to be creative and bring forth new life. That is exactly what God wants to do with those who are broken and discouraged.

And one of them, when he saw that he was healed, turned back, and with a loud voice glorified God, and fell down on his face at His feet, giving Him thanks: and he was a Samaritan. And Jesus answering said, Were there not ten cleansed? but where are the nine? There are not found that returned to give glory to God save this stranger. And He said unto him, Arise, go thy way: thy faith hath made thee whole.

Luke 17:15-19

Ten men walked like hikers on the side of the road with nothing but a Word from God. They were changed while in the process of obeying the command of a Savior whom they had called out to a few miles back on the dusty road where all miracles are walked out. Peeking beneath their clothes, checking spots that had once been afflicted, they laughed in the wind as the reality of their deliverance became even more real with every step they took. There is no success like the success of a man who had to persevere in order to receive it. People appreciate the victory when they have to walk it out.

For we are His workmanship, created in Christ Jesus unto good works, which God hath before ordained that we should walk in them.

Ephesians 2:10

If great things came from those who never suffered, we might think that they accomplished those things of their own accord. When a broken person submits to God, God gets the glory for the wonderful things He accomplishes—no matter how far that person has fallen. The anointing of God will restore you and make you accomplish great and noble things. Believe it!

The hidden Christ that's been locked up behind your fears, your problems and your insecurity, will come forth in your life. You will see the power of the Lord Jesus do a mighty thing.

After the angel spoke to Mary, she said, *"...be it unto me according to thy word."* (Luke 1:38). Not according to my marital status or my job or what I deserve—*"Be it unto me according to thy word."*

Mary knew enough to believe God and to submit to Him. She was taking an extreme risk. To be pregnant and unmarried brought dire consequences in those days. Yet she willingly gave herself over to the Lord.

If ye then, being evil, know how to give good gifts unto your children, how much more shall your Father which is in heaven give good things to them that ask Him?

Matthew 7:11

Perhaps you are one who has the discernment to know that this blessing is nothing without the One who caused it all to happen. Most people are so concerned about their immediate needs that they fail to take the powerful experience that comes from a continued relationship with God! This is for the person who goes back to the Sender of gifts with the power of praise. Many will climb the corporate ladder. Some will claim the accolades of this world. But soon all will realize that success, even with all its glamour, cannot heal a parched soul that needs the refreshment of a change of peace. Nothing can bring wholeness like the presence of God. He first blessed you to see if you would return from the temporal to embrace the eternal.

Remember, healing can be found anywhere, but wholeness is achieved only when you go back to the Sender with all of your heart and thank Him for the miracle.

Therefore if any man be in Christ, he is a new creature: old things are passed away; behold, all things are become new.

2 Corinthians 5:17

The anointing of God will restore you and make you accomplish great things. The hidden Christ that's been locked up behind your problems and your insecurity, will come forth in your life. You will see the power of the Lord Jesus do a mighty thing.

If you have had a dream, and sensed a promise, reach out to Him. Every woman who knows that they have another woman inside them who hasn't come forth can reach their hearts toward God and He will meet those inner needs and cause them to live at their potential. He will restore what was stolen by your suffering and abuse. He will take back from the enemy what was swallowed up in your history.

Satan attempts to keep us from our potential. There is great potential in those who believe. That potential may be locked up because of ruined histories. God will wipe the slate clean. He will likely use others to help in the process, but it is His anointing that will bring forth new life.

So the man gave names to all the livestock, the birds of the air and all the beasts of the field. But for Adam no suitable helper was found.

Genesis 2:20 NIV

Most of us have had the unfortunate experience of being the victim of some matchmaking friend who inappropriately sets us up with someone who doesn't quite fit the bill. The blind date can be a terribly embarrassing situation. It is very difficult for even our close friends to predict who will attract us. I can remember contemplating the decision to marry. I sought the counsel of a very close friend. Choosing a wife is one of the most personal decisions you will ever have to make—far too personal to accept the advice of people who will not have to live with the decision.

Attractions, for many people, can be as deadly as a net to a fish. Fish struggle, trying to get away, but the more they struggle, the more entangled they become. The key is not to struggle with the thing or the person. The deliverance comes from within and not from without. The victory is won within the battleground of your mind, and its memories and needs.

To whom also He showed Himself alive after His passion by many infallible proofs, being seen of them forty days, and speaking of the things pertaining to the kingdom of God.

Acts 1:3

Perhaps it is no coincidence that the Greek word *pathos*, usually translated as "suffer" or "to feel," is used to describe Christ's crucifixion. What a strange choice of expression for such a hideous occurrence. Yet it alludes to a deeper truth that each of us must face. Although the inference is toward His suffering, look a little deeper beneath the sufferings that He experienced and understand that there was an underlying ecstasy beneath the pain of the Cross. The writer of Hebrews alludes to it as he lifts the veil and peeks behind the crisis of the Cross and reports the purpose of the Cross.

There can be no fulfillment where there is no passion. The passion that causes us to achieve has to be strong enough to make us uncomfortable. The discomfort that comes from the desire must be intense enough to keep the obstacles between you and the thing you desire from aborting the intensity of your desire!

She shall be called Woman, because she was taken out of Man.

Genesis 2:23b

The first female mentioned in the Bible was created mature, without a childhood or an example to define her role and relationship to her husband. The first female was created a woman while Adam was asleep. That the Lord "brought her to the man" is the first hint of marriage. I believe it would be better if we still allowed God to bring to us what He has for us. The only biblical evolution I can find is the woman, who evolved out of man. She is God's gift to man. When God wanted to be praised, He created man in His own likeness and in His image. Likewise, God gave man someone like himself. Adam said that she is *"bone of my bones, and flesh of my flesh"* (Gen. 2:23). His attraction to her was her likeness to him. He called her "womb man" or woman. Like the Church of Christ, Eve was his Body and his Bride.

For this cause shall a man leave his father and mother, and shall be joined unto his wife, and they two shall be one flesh (Ephesians 5:31).

And God said, "Let the land produce living crea-
tures according to their kinds: livestock, creatures
that move along the ground, and wild animals, each
according to its kind...."

Genesis 1:24 NIV

We are communal by nature; we have a strong need for community and relationships. However, whatever we are in relationship with, we also are related to. It is important that we do not covenant with someone or something with which we are not really related. Every living being was created to pursue and cohabit with its own kind. I emphasize *kind*. There should be an agreement in species to achieve maximum compatibility.

Hence, we are forbidden from seeking intimacy, which is a legitimate need, from an inappropriate source. This is a biological law that governs biological order. Whether or not a man is Christian, this law is still in effect. He can break it, but its penalties would be incomprehensible. What was introduced in the shadow of Old Testament theology as a biological law is magnified in the New Testament as a spiritual reality. Why? The Church is a species separate from any other, a species of which Christ is the firstborn.

> But now they desire a better country, that is, an
> heavenly: wherefore God is not ashamed to be called
> their God: for He hath prepared for them a city.
>
> *Hebrews 11:16*

There can be no fulfillment where there is no passion. It is the force of your personal passion to achieve that gives you the force to break down the wall between you and the thing you desire.

Jesus, our prime example of success, had a cross between Him and His goal. The Cross was not the end; it was the means. He didn't enjoy the means, but He endured it—His passion was for the end. What gave Him the power to endure, His means to achieve the end, was His passion.

There is an intense discomfort associated with passion and desire. Have you ever noticed that God mightily uses some of the most wretched sinners whom He converted into great ministers? It is because these were people who were accustomed to passion and acquisition. They were people who dared to desire. They were people who, although misdirected at one time, possessed such a burning passion that, if bridled and directed, could make them people of great accomplishment.

But from the beginning of the creation God made
them male and female. For this cause shall a man
leave his father and mother, and cleave to his wife.
Mark 10:6-7

Man and woman were made of the same material. Adam says, "She is bone of my bone." When you find a person with whom you are compatible, there is a bonding that consummates marriage that has nothing to do with sex. I also understand how you could feel this person to be the only choice in the world. Everyone you meet isn't bone of your bone! It is important that you do not allow anyone to manipulate you into choosing someone with whom you have no bond. Everyone must pray and discern if the other is someone they could cleave to the rest of their life.

The term "cleave" is translated from the Hebrew word *debaq*. It means "to impinge, cling or adhere to; figuratively, to catch by pursuit or follow close after." There is a great need in most of our lives to cleave, to feel that sense of belonging. It is a knitting together of two thirsty hearts at the oasis of a loving commitment.

Be ye not unequally yoked together with unbelievers: for what fellowship hath righteousness with unrighteousness? and what communion hath light with darkness?

2 Corinthians 6:14

We believers are told not to be unequally yoked with unbelievers. We are twice-born people; we are born and then born again. Now, it is not biologically illegal for us to bond with unbelievers; it is spiritually illegal. To be a sinner is to be dead in sin!

As physical death is separation of the spirit and the body, so spiritual death, the state sinners are in, is the spirit of man separated from relationship with his Creator. Like Adam, he is hiding in the bushes of sin and covering himself with the fig leaves of excuses.

In the Scriptures, death doesn't mean the cessation of life. It means separation. When a person dies physically, it is not the end of life; it is merely the separation of the body from the spirit.

Sin is separation of relationship with God, but the eternal separation from the presence of God is hell. The good news is: *"And you hath He quickened, who were dead in trespasses and sins"* (Eph. 2:1).

Delight thyself also in the Lord; and He shall give thee the desires of thine heart. Commit thy way unto the Lord; trust also in Him; and He shall bring it to pass.

Psalm 37:4-5

Oh, thou man or woman of great passion, driven by intense feelings and desire, you often wrestle with your ambitious nature. Hear me and hear me well: You don't want to kill your passion; you just need to redirect it toward a godly vision. That is why satan has desired to have you. He knows that if you ever line up your passion with God's purpose, you will become a spiritual dynamo. Then there will be no stopping you until the flames of your passion are quenched in the streams of your eternal destiny!

Do not resent your passion. Control it, yes, but please don't kill it. Without it, you would be as limp as an over-cooked noodle, your life as bland as hospital food. God created you to be zesty and alive! Even though you may have often misdirected your passions, allow God to recycle your feelings. Retrieve your passions from your dusty religious receptacle and place them in God's recycling program!

And they twain shall be one flesh: so then they are
no more twain, but one flesh.

Mark 10:8

Marriage is so personal that no one will be able to stand outside your relationship and see why you bond with that person. If you are married, understand that your spouse isn't running for office. He shouldn't have to meet the approval of all your family and friends. To cleave is to stick together. Have you made the commitment to stay together? The secret to cleaving is leaving. *"For this cause shall a man leave his father and mother..."* (Mark 10:7).

If you enter into marriage and still keep other options open, whether mental, emotional or physical, it will never work. When the tugging of adversity tries the bonds of your matrimony, you will fall apart. You must leave and cleave to your spouse. It is so unhealthy to cleave to someone other than your spouse for support. Now we all need wholesome friendships. However, none should have more influence over you than your spouse (after God). Some of you could save your marriages if you would leave some of these extra-marital ties and cleave to your companion!

*The thief cometh not, but for to steal, and to kill,
and to destroy: I am come that they might have
life, and that they might have it more abundantly.*

John 10:10

When you are in sin, you reach after anything that
will numb the pain and help you forget that something is missing. You can be reconciled to God at this
very moment! The Bible says that you were dead in the
trespass of sin (see Eph. 2:1). It teaches that you, as well
as all of us, were separated from God because of sin. But
God has reconciled His people to Himself. Being
reunited with Him means you have abundant life.

To be willfully disobedient and choose a companion who
is dead in the trespasses of sin, is to be involved in spiritual necrophilia. I am not referring to those who, while
still a sinner, married another sinner, and then were converted. I am concerned for those who find themselves
attracted to others who haven't had this born-again experience. The person who willingly chooses to ignore
God's stop signs is bound to experience adversity. It's not
His will for the living to marry the dead!

*Who can find a virtuous woman? for her price is
far above rubies.*

Proverbs 31:10

Believe God for your marriage! It will not be your
feelings that heal your relationship; it will be your
faith. Did you know that you cannot trust your own feelings? I counsel people all the time who sit with tears
streaming down their weary faces and say, "I just can't
trust him." I've got news for you. You can't trust yourself
either! Your feelings will swing in and out. But your faith
will not move.

There is a certain way a woman treats a man when she is
fulfilled. It takes faith to treat a marriage that is frustrating with the same respect you would treat the prosperous
relationship. I am simply saying many times you feel
yourself holding back who you would like to be so you
can maintain this strong exterior. If you suppress who
you are, you will fall into depression! It is terrible to
arrest who you are in an attempt to "fight fire with fire."
The best way to fight fire is with water! The winning
way of a woman is not in her words, it is in her character.

*And that, knowing the time, that now it is high
time to awake out of sleep: for now is our salvation
nearer than when we believed.*

Romans 13:11

What good is life without living? Taste it, live it—
even at the risk of occasional failure and adversity!
Have you any passion to triumph? Your desire to protect
yourself from further disappointment has placed you in a
comatose state. Wake up and play! You are not dead!
There may be many things about you that are dead, but
you are not dead!

You wanted to make a difference, but since you ran into
some obstacle, some cross, you decided to adjust your
expectations to your limitations and just keep smiling!

You are wrong! I am blowing a trumpet loudly into your
rigor mortis-ridden ear! God has too much for you to do!
Arise, breathe deeply of this moment. There will never
be another moment in your life like this one! I can't
spare you tears, fears, or traumas; each passion has its
"cross of validation." In fact, it is the Cross that validates
the enormity of the passion. It is what you endure that
expresses how deeply you desire.

> *Wives, in the same way be submissive to your husbands so that, if any of them do not believe the word, they may be won over without words....*
>
> 1 Peter 3:1 NIV

While teaching a seminar, a lady raised her hand and said, "I am a widow. I lost my husband and he died unsaved." She was obviously wrestling with grief as she spoke. She continued, "I claimed First Peter 3:1 and at the end of his life he still was not saved." I responded, "That scripture doesn't mean that the responsibility of getting the husband saved rests on the wife. It just says that a submissive, quiet woman creates an atmosphere so he may be won."

I rebuked the condemning spirit of guilt and she worshiped God under the anointing of the Holy Spirit. This passage of Peter's is not given to abuse women; it is given to instruct them about what works well in the home. Faith is not loud and fleshly; it is quiet and spiritual. No one can do anything to make another person be saved. But you can create an atmosphere where your conduct is not undermining your prayers!

Remember that at that time you were separate from Christ…But now in Christ Jesus you who once were far away have been brought near through the blood of Christ.

Ephesians 2:12-13

W ho would walk past a casket in a funeral home and wink at a corpse? The very idea wavers between being disgusting and hilarious! What type of mind could not grasp the fact that this is inappropriate behavior for intelligent human beings? No widower would take his deceased wife out for a final weekend of romance. Romancing a stone? I should think not!

If this whole idea is so terrible, and it is, then why would born-again Christians who have been made alive by the power of God, go back into their own past and rummage through the graveyard of circumstances that God says are dead and over with? Why continue to embrace what ought to be buried? Regardless of how alive the event was at the time, when God says it is dead, then it is dead! How strange it must be in the spirit world for you, a living soul, to be wrapped up with a dead issue you have not yet relinquished.

...but by love serve one another.

Galatians 5:13b

Women tend to be vocal while men tend to be physical. Women feel that everything needs to be discussed. Men communicate through touch. It is terrible to be misunderstood! I am a giver. Whenever I feel affection, I want to buy a gift for my wife. Although my wife will acknowledge the gifts, she will go into orbit over cards! We spent the first few years of our marriage teaching each other our language.

Your spouse may really think he's telling you something that you keep complaining about not getting. He feels like, "What more does she want? I told her that I married her. I did this and that and the other." You may be living in the Tower of Babel. That was the place where families divided because they could not understand each other's language. Sit down and learn each other's language before frustration turns your house into the Tower of Babel. At Babel all work ceased and arguing began. If you are arguing, it is because frustration exists between you. People who don't care don't argue. No one argues over what they would rather leave!

For God so loved the world, that He gave His only begotten Son, that whosoever believeth in Him should not perish, but have everlasting life.

John 3:16

He "so loved" us. That's what He did on the Cross. This passionate lover, whose Kingdom was not of this world, came to our world and, with unfeigned love, reached into the jaws of damnation and caught my falling soul. His love is exemplified in His coming, but it is consummated in His dying. In His living He betrothed us, but in His dying He procured us.

Jesus Christ, the greatest lover the world has ever known, gives Himself openly and unashamedly. He has found in the Cross a mode of expression that becomes a picture of the magnitude of His love. His suffering was a by-product of His passion.

Where there is no passion, there simply is no power. I fear greatly that the enemy will attempt to either steal the passion or smother it beneath the fear of failure and rejection. If we exist without passion, we slump into a state of stagnation that hinders us from achieving the purpose of God in our lives.

Likewise, ye wives, be in subjection to your own husbands; that, if any obey not the word, they also may without the word be won by the conversation of the wives.

1 Peter 3:1

Married women—when you approach your husband, do not corner him. Catch him at a time when he won't feel interrogated. You would be surprised at how men tend to avoid open confrontation. Even men who are physically abusive still have moments when they feel anxiety about facing their wives.

Men's communication is different. I am not suggesting that men can't learn the communication method of their wives. I am merely saying that spouses must learn to appreciate each other's language. Remember, I briefly discussed faith for your marriage. Faith calls those things that are not as though they were.

Everything you were going to do for him when he changes, do it now and do it by faith. Then God will turn your Tower of Babel into a Pentecost! At Pentecost each person heard the message in their own language (see Acts 2:6). I pray that God would interpret the language of your spouse and that your love be fruitful and productive.

And what concord hath Christ with Belial? or what part hath he that believeth with an infidel? And what agreement hath the temple of God with idols? for ye are the temple of the living God; as God hath said, I will dwell in them, and walk in them; and I will be their God, and they shall be My people.

2 Corinthians 6:15-16

Whether we admit it or not, we know that an unholy alliance cannot produce holy matrimony. No, the subtle serpent has gone deeper than that! He has many wonderful, well-meaning Christians praising, worshiping, and going to church, but in the stillness of the night, when no one is around, they lie in bed in the privacy of their homes, pull out guilt, scars, and memories, and play with the dead. If it's dead—and it is—then bury it!

Release the pain from the memory. The link that keeps you tied to what is past must be broken. I agree with you right now in the name of Jesus that those unsettled and unsettling issues that keep holding you in the night and affecting you in the light are broken by the power of God!

Above all else, guard your heart, for it is the well-spring of life.

Proverbs 4:23 NIV

———————

Be aware that the enemy is trying to steal something from you that is not visible. Any time the invisible is stolen, its absence is not readily detected. On what day does passion leave a marriage? On which morning did the worker lose interest in his job? At what point does the customer decide, "I am not going to buy the product"?

The only solution lies in the absolute, committed guarding of the heart. Your greatest treasure isn't your certificate of deposit. It isn't your retirement, or your stocks and bonds. Your greatest treasure is in the strength of the passion that is locked in the recesses of your heart. Out of the heart flow the issues of life.

You must keep a firm sobriety about you, warming your heart with it like it was a warm coat on a wintry night. Keep a sobriety that refuses to become drunken with fear, discontentment, or insecurity. Wrap your godly attitude closely around your heart, for it is the wellspring or the resource from which comes the strength to keep on living and giving!

And the Lord God called unto Adam, and said unto him, Where art thou? And he said, I heard Thy voice in the garden, and I was afraid, because I was naked; and I hid myself.

Genesis 3:9-10

Marriage is at its best when both parties can be naked and not be ashamed. It is important that your husband be able to take it off, to take it all off. There is no resting place for the man who hides in his own house. The Lord asked Adam, *"Where art thou?"* When men are restored to their rightful place in the home, the family will come out of chaos.

Listen as Adam exposes the tendency of most men to avoid open confrontation. These are the four points of his confession: (1) I heard Thy voice. (2) I was afraid. (3) I was naked. (4) I hid myself. When you become confrontational, it's not that men don't hear you. But when men become afraid or exposed (naked), they have a tendency to hide.

Marriage needs to be transparent. Both you and your spouse need to be able to expose your vulnerabilities without fear or condemnation.

How shall we, that are dead to sin, live any longer therein? Know ye not, that so many of us as were baptized into Jesus Christ were baptized into His death? Therefore we are buried with Him by baptism into death: that like as Christ was raised up from the dead by the glory of the Father, even so we also should walk in newness of life.

Romans 6:2b-4

Be careful what you allow to become one with you. You cannot continue to live in the past. Break away from the intimate contact it would have on your life. Some things might never get resolved. They are like zombies walking around inside you all your life. Enough is enough! Everything that will not be healed must be forsaken. Really, to forsake it is to forget it. You cannot live in an intertwining embrace with something that God says you are to reckon as dead! Do not yield your body, your time, or your strength to this phantom lover! Tell that old corpse, "You can't touch this!"

"Likewise reckon ye also yourselves to be dead indeed unto sin, but alive unto God through Jesus Christ our Lord."

Romans 6:11

But by the grace of God I am what I am, and His grace toward me was not in vain; but I labored more abundantly than they all, yet not I but the grace of God which was with me.

1 Corinthians 15:10 NKJV

You can't spend the rest of your life trying to protect yourself from the struggles of life. Look at the birthing table of the expectant mother. It is designed to hold her in the birth position in spite of the pain. Can you maintain your position—even when it means that you will be exposed to a harsh level of pain? That is what good ministry does in our lives. It holds us in place, even when we would have stepped out of the will of God to save ourselves from the stress of the process.

Jesus was tied to the birthing table in the garden of Gethsemane. The Church was in Him "from the foundation of the world," and it was to be brought out of His bleeding side on the Cross. As the pains became greater, He prayed to change position. He didn't want to be in the vulnerable position of delivery!

> *For the lips of a strange woman drop as an honey-comb, and her mouth is smoother than oil: but her end is bitter as wormwood, sharp as a two-edged sword.*
>
> *Proverbs 5:3-4*

I want to share something with you that may sound unorthodox. I pray it will bless someone. I want to stop by Delilah's house (see Judg. 16:4-20). Most women would not want to stop at her house; most men would! Most men are not afraid of Delilah; most women do not like her. Her morals are inexcusable, but her methods are worth discussing. There are some things that every wife could learn, must learn, from Delilah. The Bible says nothing about her appearance. Her clothing, makeup, or hairdo are not mentioned. What was it about this woman that was so powerful? What was it that attracted and captivated the attention of this mighty man, Samson? What was it about this woman that kept drawing him back to her? What was it that made Samson keep going back to her even when he knew she was trying to kill him? He could not leave her alone—he desperately needed her. It is a "fatal attraction" in the Old Testament!

What a wretched man I am! Who will rescue me from this body of death?

Romans 7:24 NIV

Paul uses these terms to declare his struggles because he is wrestling with a corpse. This nauseating level of intimacy with mushy flesh would turn the strongest stomach. That is exactly how Paul felt about the old nature that continued to press in so closely to his existence—rubbing him, touching him, always reminding him of things he could neither change nor eradicate.

Eventually, for the punished murderer, this bacteria-filled, murky, mushy flesh would pass its fungus and disease to him until he died from this association with the dead. What an agonizing, disgusting way to die. When the apostle realized that his association with his past was affecting his present, he cried out, "O wretched man that I am! Who shall deliver me from so great a death?" No one was worthy to answer the call. The cry searched the earth—past, present, and future—and found a bleeding Lamb and an empty tomb. Then the angels cried, "Worthy is the Lamb! He is so worthy. Let Him untie you from this curse and be healed!"

> *Confess your faults one to another, and pray one for*
> *another, that ye may be healed. The effective fervent*
> *prayer of a righteous man availeth much.*
>
> *James 5:16*

We are tied to our destiny like a little trembling lamb is tied to the altar for sacrifice. Like a woman lifted to the birthing bed, trembling in pain, forehead drenched with perspiration—we who are on the verge of miracles are always kept in a perpetual state of vulnerability! If it were not for our passion for an expected end, we would have just fainted away entirely, declaring that the process is too great and the reward too insignificant.

There has to be a certain intensity of desire to empower a person to persevere. Even when we pray, God isn't moved by our vocabulary. He has answered the broken, fragmented prayers of the illiterate mind, whose limited intellect could not abort the childlike faith that produces miracles. He is, as the Scriptures declare, *"touched with the feeling of our infirmities"* (Heb. 4:15). The passionate God is, in fact, touched by the passions of the prayers of the infirm.

We need God's mercies newly bestowed upon us every morning.

And beheld among the simple ones, I discerned among the youths, a young man void of under-standing...behold, there met him a woman with the attire of a harlot, and subtle of heart....With her much fair speech she caused him to yield, with the flattering of her lips she forced him.

Proverbs 7:7,10,21

This discussion is for women married to men working in high-stress positions—men who are powerful and full of purpose. Jesus described well the problem of highly motivated men. Jesus said, *"Foxes have holes, and birds of the air have nests; but the Son of man hath not where to lay His head"* (Luke 9:58). Where can the mighty man lay his head or become vulnerable? Where can he take off his armor and rest for a few hours? He doesn't want to quit; he merely needs to rest. Is your home a restful place to be? Is it clean and neat? Is it warm and inviting?

Men, created in the likeness of God, respond to praise. A woman who knows what to say to a man is difficult to withstand. For all men's tears and all their fears, they need your arms, your words, your song.

It is a faithful saying: for if we be dead with Him,
we shall also live with Him: if we suffer, we shall
also reign with Him: if we deny Him, He also will
deny us: if we believe not, yet He abideth faithful:
He cannot deny Himself.

2 Timothy 2:11-13

You can live with those dead things hanging and clinging to you no better than Paul could. Allow the transforming power of God to rush through your life and cut the cord between you and your past. Whatever you do, remember to get rid of the old body. If the past is over, there is no need for you to walk around with mummies on your back—or on your mind! Get rid of that body and do it now! Those old memories will try to negotiate a deal, but you don't need a twin hanging on you. You don't need a secret affair with a corpse. You don't even need it as a roommate.

This is the time for an epitaph, not a revival. There are some things in life you will want to revive, but not this one. The past is something you want to die.

Now therefore ye are no more strangers and for-
eigners, but fellow citizens with the saints, and of
the household of God; and are built upon the foun-
dation of the apostles and prophets, Jesus Christ
Himself being the chief corner stone.

Ephesians 2:19-20

By God's design, left splayed before us on the pages of the Scriptures, are the intricate details of the life of David, whose passions were both an asset and a liability. His inner struggles and childhood dysfunctions are openly aired on the pages of the text like the center fold-out in a tabloid.

God displayed David's failures to give us a point of reference that exhibits the manifold grace of God. How marvelous is the message that instructs us that if God could use a David, He also can use us, as we are all men of like passions.

Did you know that God used men who were similarly affected (as you are) by certain stimuli and struggles? What a joy to know that treasure can be surrounded by trash and still not lose its value! Is a diamond less valuable if it is found in a clogged drain? Of course not!

There is difference also between a wife and a virgin. The unmarried woman careth for the things of the Lord, that she may be holy both in body and in spirit: but she that is married careth for the things of the world, how she may please her husband.

1 Corinthians 7:34

Marriage is a ministry. Love is centered on giving, not taking. Marriage is so much a ministry that the apostle Paul teaches the married woman she cannot afford to become so spiritual that she is unavailable for the ministry of marriage. The Greek word used there for "careth" means to be anxious about or to have intense concern. Married woman need to be concerned about pleasing their husbands. Your ministry, as a wife, begins not in the mall, but in your own home and to your own spouse. Now, I am certainly not implying that a woman should be locked in the kitchen and chained to the bed! I am sharing that priorities need to start in the home and then spread to careers, vocations, and ministerial pursuits. For the woman who "careth for," God will anoint you to be successful in the ministry of marriage.

And you hath He quickened, who were dead in tres-
passes and sins; wherein in time past ye walked
according to the course of this world, according to
the prince of the power of the air, the spirit that now
worketh in the children of disobedience.

Ephesians 2:1-2

There are some things you would like to have removed extremely far away. There are things I would like to lay to rest in such a definite way that they become merely fleeting wisps of fog faintly touching the recesses of the mind—gone, over, finished! It is those dearly departed, ghostly, painful issues of which I wrote. These phantom assassins are not to be trifled with; they must be laid to rest! This funeral, my friend, is not for them— it is you who must know it's over. Gather together all those villainous ghosts that desecrate the sanctity of what God would do in your life. Examine them. Cry if need be; scream if necessary—but when the service is over, bury every incident in the freshly turned soil of this Word from God. Know that God has delivered you from playing with dead things.

Keep back thy servant also from presumptuous sins; let them not have dominion over me: then shall I be upright, and I shall be innocent from the great transgression.

Psalm 19:13

The same passion that makes us very good could potentially make us very bad. Undirected passion becomes a spawning bed for perversity and dankness. It is what we do with what we feel that controls the direction of our lives. The same sail that causes a ship to run before an eastward wind can also push it headlong in another direction.

Passions are to be submitted to the Father, just as our Lord submitted His all on the Cross. That is the place where He wielded all of His passion—His passion was aimed at the joy set before Him, the target of being a submitted Son. God tested the power of committed passion at Calvary. If it had not been effective, Christ would have had to buy Joseph's tomb instead of borrow it. This is frightening if you read this with the mummy-like mentality that preempts most people from accomplishing anything. They neutralize their passion with an apathy and unconcern that renders them flaccid and ineffective.

Marriage is honourable in all, and the bed unde-filed: but whoremongers and adulterers God will judge.

Hebrews 13:4

There will be no marriages in Heaven (see Matt. 22:30). Marriage is for this world. Inasmuch as it is a worldly institution, married people cannot divorce themselves from the "things of the world." Notice this definition of the Greek word *kosmos* translated as "world" which implies that there should be a concern for a harmonious order in the house. God gives the gift of marriage, but you must do your own decorating. Decorate your relationship or it will become bland for you and for your spouse. Decoration does not come where there is no concern.

You have a ministry to your companion. The Scripture didn't say married women were to be carnal. It just sets some priorities. Where there are no priorities, there is a sense of being overwhelmed by responsibility. You can still consecrate yourself as long as you are a companion to your spouse. God has ascribed honor to marriage. However you choose to decorate your relationship is holy. Do not neglect each other in the name of being spiritual. God wants you to be together!

So we fix our eyes not on what is seen, but on what is unseen. For what is seen is temporary, but what is unseen is eternal.

2 Corinthians 4:18 NIV

Mozart, one of the great composers of all time, sat late at night writing what was to be a masterpiece of symphonic excellence. He decided to stop and go to bed. Strangely, once he was in bed, he found sleep evasive. His work continued churning around in his mind. You see, he had ended the symphony with an augmented chord. An augmented chord gives the feeling of waiting on something else to be heard.

Finally, when this composer could stand it no longer, he rose and stumbled down the steps. He went through all that to write one note. Yet how important that note was. It gave a sense of ending to the piece, and so was worth getting out of bed to write. People can never rest while living in a suspended mode. This composer placed the quill back on his desk and triumphantly retraced his way up the stairs. He slipped into the bed with a feeling of satisfaction. For him, the struggle was over.

The husband should fulfill his marital duty to his wife, and likewise the wife to her husband. The wife's body does not belong to her alone but also to her husband. In the same way, the husband's body does not belong to him alone but also to his wife. Do not deprive each other except by mutual consent and for a time, so that you may devote yourselves to prayer....

1 Corinthians 7:3-5

If you are looking for someone to be your everything, don't look around, look up! God is the only One who can be everything. By expecting perfection from the flesh, you ask more out of someone else than what you can provide yourself. To be married is to have a partner: someone who is not always there or always on target or always anything!

On the other hand, should you ever get in trouble, you can count on your partner! It is having someone who is as concerned as you are when your children are ill. To be married is to have someone's shoulder to cry on. As the curtain closes on all you have attempted to do and be; you will see someone to whom you mattered!

Unto the woman He said, I will geatly multiply thy sorrow and thy conception; in sorrow thou shalt bring forth children; and thy desire shall be to thy husband, and he shall rule over thee.

Genesis 3:16

When God spoke to the first woman about childbirth, He spoke of sorrow and travail. He spoke of the violent, tempestuous pain of labor. He forewarned her about the billowing progression of contractions she would experience at the end of the third trimester of pregnancy. Her pelvic bones are literally moved apart, as if separated by the effects of an earthquake. The near-deathlike pains come faster and harder as she gets closer to delivery. Afterward, you would expect her to vow never to know another man again!

However, God says that at the end of all this labor and pain, He would recycle the relationship between the woman and the man by the return of desire! God knows that there is no cure for past pain like present desire. If the desire is strong enough, the pain of the past will dissipate. The wounded and the weary will rise victoriously with new desire, and the cycle continues.

He brought me to the banqueting house, and his banner over me was love.

Song of Solomon 2:4

————

I hope you can relate to what a blessing it is to be alive, to be able to feel, to be able to taste life. Lift the glass to your mouth and drink deeply of life; it is a privilege to experience every drop of a human relationship. It is not perfect; but the imperfection adds to its uniqueness. I am sure yours, like mine, is a mixing of good days, sad days, and all the challenges of life. I hope you have learned that a truly good relationship is filled with dreams and pains and tender moments. Moments that make you smile secret smiles in the middle of the day. Moments so strong that they never die, but yet are so fragile they disappear like bubbles in a glass. It does not matter whether you have something to be envied or something to be developed; if you can look back and catch a few moments, you are blessed! You could have been anywhere doing anything but instead the maitre d' has seated you at a *table for two!*

And wisdom and knowledge shall be the stability of thy times, and strength of salvation: the fear of the Lord is His treasure.

Isaiah 33:6

There ought to be a threefold celebration going on in your heart right now. First, you ought to look back over your times of obscurity, when He was plowing and fertilizing you, and thank God that you are still here to attest to His sustaining power. A lesser vessel would not have survived your testimony.

Second, look around you at the blessings that you have right now. With a twinkle in your eye and a melody in your heart, thank God for what He is doing even at this moment. Your freshly cultivated ground is full of seeds and unborn potential.

Third, you should celebrate what God is about to do in your life. Your heart ought to be thumping in your chest; your blood ought to be racing like a car engine about to peel rubber! You are about to step into the greatest harvest of your life. You were created for this moment—and this moment was created for you! Do you know what time it is? It's your time!

And supper being ended, the devil having now put into the heart of Judas Isacariot, Simon's son, to betray Him; Jesus knowing that the Father had given all things into His hands, and that He was come from God, and went to God; He riseth from supper, and laid aside His garments; and took a towel and girded Himself. After that He poureth water into a basin, and began to wash the disciples' feet....

John 13:2-5

Supper is over and the dishes are cleared away. We have had a "reality check" through the unveiling of Judas. We now realize that our ultimate purpose for gathering isn't really for fellowship. He gathers us to sharpen us through our attempts at fellowship. He often prunes us through the people with whom we worship. They become the utensils the Lord uses to perfect those whom He has called. It is only a matter of time before they begin the stage-by-stage unmasking and realize that the dinner guests have more flaws than you have ever imagined! The only spotless splendor is the Host Himself—all others are merely patients; just mutilated, torn, dilapidated, disfigured caricatures of social grace and ambiance.

Are not two sparrows sold for a farthing? And one of them shall not fall on the ground without your Father. But the very hairs of your head are all numbered. Fear ye not therefore, ye are of more value than many sparrows.

Matthew 10:29-31

No scientist has ever been able to make a woman. No doctor has been able to create a woman. No engineer has been able to build a woman. However, God has made fine women. You don't have to look like a TV commercial model to be beautiful.

We must learn to thank God for who we are. If God had wanted you to look like someone else, He would have made you like that. God will send somebody along who will appreciate you the way you are.

Remind yourself, "I am valuable to God. I am somebody. And I won't let another use me and abuse me and treat me like I'm nothing. Yes, I've been through some bad times. I've been hurt and I've been bent out of shape, but the Lord touched me and loosed me and now I am glorifying God and I'm not going back to where I came from."

Then said He also to him that bade Him, When thou makest a dinner of a supper, call not thy friends, not thy brethren, neither thy kinsmen, not thy rich neighbors; lest they also bid thee again, and a recompense be made thee. But when thou makest a feast, call the poor, the maimed, the lame, the blind: and thou shalt be blessed; for they cannot recompense thee: for thou shalt be recompensed at the resurrection of the just.

Luke 14:12-14

These harsh realities are merely a semblance of what we gradually encounter as we face the rude awakenings of ministry. We learn to understand Peter's anger and his occasional tendency to lie. We feel the constant insecurities of Thomas, whose doubtful warnings seem to come against every attempt we would make toward progress. We encounter the painful betrayal of our old friend, Judas Iscariot, whose twisted way of loving us never seems to stop him from killing us.

When we see Jesus, we can only sit in splendor and thank God that He is gracious enough to invite the impaired and the impoverished—lest the very seat in which we sit be emptied as well!

If thou put the brethren in remembrance of these things, thou shalt be a good minister of Jesus Christ, nourished up in the words of faith and of good doctrine, whereunto thou hast attained.

1 Timothy 4:6

There is a time when we must move beyond supper-time. We must move beyond the stage in our development where we come to a ministry just to be fed, where our whole focus for coming to the table is always to receive. We must make the transition that every believer must make—some call it the transition from believership to discipleship, but I just call it the transition from suppertime to service time.

God only opens your eyes so you can get up from the table and give someone else a turn in the seat. It is time for you to learn the art of service and move beyond supper.

Are we still sitting around the cluttered dishes of dead programs whose crushed crumbs are not enough to feed this impoverished age? Even the waiter has gone home, and here we sit, rehearsing the same excuses! We need men and women who will rise from supper.

Whose adorning let it not be that outward adorning of plaiting the hair, and of wearing of gold, or of putting on of apparel; but let it be the hidden man of the heart, in that which is not corruptible, even the ornament of a meek and quiet spirit, which is in the sight of God of great price.

1 Peter 3:3-4

Beauty and sex appeal are not the areas to concentrate on. When you focus on the wrong areas, you don't get the right results. Society teaches you today that if you have the right hair, the right face, the right shape, and the right clothes, then you will get the right man, have the right children, and live happily ever after. That is simply not true. Life is not a fairy tale.

God put some things into the feminine spirit that a man needs more than anything God put on the feminine body. If a woman knows who she is on the inside, no matter what she looks like, she will have no problem being attractive to a man. If she knows her own self-worth, then when she comes before that man, he will receive her.

He riseth from supper, and laid aside His garments;
and took a towel and girded Himself. After that He
poureth water into a basin, and began to wash the
disciples' feet, and to wipe them with the towel
wherewith He was girded.

John 13:4-5

Jesus taught a powerful lesson about ministry as He rose from supper and began to disrobe in front of men who were still clothed. Isn't our problem the fact that we don't want to be seen as the only one? The fear of being different can lock you in a vault. It can close you in a prison of disobedience because you are afraid of being alone.

We will never have real ministry until someone changes the atmosphere in our boring little conferences and conventions. Real ministry will start the moment we stop trying to impress each other and say, "Look! This is how I really look beneath my name, my reputation, or my success. This is who I really am!"

Jesus paid the price. He took the leap that few would ever dare to take. He laid aside His garments before those whom He had labored to inspire. Yet we have not followed His example.

But it shall not be so among you: but whosoever
will be great among you, let him be your minister;
and whosoever will be chief among you, let him be
your servant: even as the Son of man came not to be
ministered unto, but to minister, and to give His
life a ransom for many.

Matthew 20:26-28

We are still squirming and fuming over exposing, forgiving, and washing one another's feet! We need the whole of us cleansed! We have never accepted people in the Church. We take in numbers and we teach them to project an image, but we have never allowed people—real people—to find a place at our table!

Hear me, my friend; we too are running out of time! We have a generation before us that has not been moved by our lavish banquets or by the glamorous buildings we have built.

Someone, quick! Tell us who you really are beneath your churchy look and your pious posture. Tell us something that makes us comfortable with our own nudity. We have carefully hidden our struggles and paraded only our victories, but the whole country is falling asleep at the parade!

Favor is deceitful, and beauty is vain: but a woman that feareth the Lord, she shall be praised.

Proverbs 31:30

The enemy wants you to be so focused on your outer appearance that you won't recognize your inner beauty, your inner strength, your inner glory. Your real value cannot be bought, applied, added on, hung from your ears, or laid on your neck. Your real strength is more than outward apparel and adornment for men. This real thing that causes a man to need you so desperately he can't leave you is not what is on you, but what is in you.

You need to recognize what God has put in you. God, when He made the woman, didn't just decorate the outside. He decorated the inside of the woman. He put beauty in her spirit.

The Scriptures talk about not having the outward adornment of gold, silver, and costly array. The Church took that passage and declared that there could be no jewelry, no makeup, and no clothing of certain types. We were so busy dealing with the negative that we didn't hear the positive of what God said. God said that He had adorned the woman inwardly.

> *When the priests enter therein, then shall they not go out of the holy place into the outer court, but there they shall lay their garments wherein they minister; for they are holy; and shall put on other garments, and shall approach to those things which are for the people.*
>
> Ezekiel 42:14

Ministry is birthed when you are stripped down to your heart's desire. You want your life to have counted for something for God.

Have you ever prayed the kind of prayer that pleads, "Oh God, don't let me impress anyone else but the One to whom I gave my life"? Have we given our lives to the Lord? Why have we not laid aside our garments?

The garment represents different things to different people. It is whatever camouflages our realness, whatever hinders us from really affecting our environment. Our garments are the personal agendas that we have set for ourselves (many of which God was never consulted about). Like the fig leaves sewn together in the garden, we have contrived our own coverings. The terrible tragedy of it all is that, sooner or later, whatever we have sown together will ultimately be stripped away.

She girdeth her loins with strength, and strengthened her arms.

Proverbs 31:17

While they behold your chaste conversation coupled with fear.

1 Peter 3:2

Understand that the word *conversation* there refers to lifestyle. You will not win a man through lip-service; you will win him through your lifestyle. He will see how you are, not what you say. He will watch how you act. He will watch your attitude. He will watch your disposition. A real problem for women believers today is that with the same mouth they use to witness to their husbands, they often curse others. You cannot witness to and win a man while he sits up and listens to you gossip about others.

Wives can win a husband by reverencing him. Woman's beauty and strength are not on the outside. There is more to you than clothes. There's more to you than gold. There's more to you than hairdos.

Society promotes the notion that beauty is found in these outer things. However, if you keep working only on these outer things, you will find yourself looking in the mirror to find your value.

Then Job arose, and rent his mantle, and shaved his head, and fell down upon the ground, and worshipped, and said, Naked came I out of my mother's womb, and naked shall I return thither: the Lord gave, and the Lord hath taken away; blessed be the name of the Lord. In all this Job dinned not, nor charged God foolishly.

Job 1:20-22

Job discusses this terrible stripping that seems to be characteristic of the call. He used to be very successful, but now he is naked and sick. His home is in shambles, his marriage is a joke, and his children—his precious children—are dead.

What word of wisdom falls from his encrusted lips? What grain of comfort does he afford himself in the vanity of his own thoughts? His only shade beneath the blistering sun of adverse circumstances is found in the fact that he can only be stripped down to what he started with. He can be stripped of the temporal, but not the eternal.

Some things you never have to lose. I'm not talking about friends, wealth, or fame. Character, class, and Christianity are three things that can survive the strippings of life!

But the Lord said unto Samuel, Look not on his
countenance, or on the height of his stature, because
I have refused him: for the Lord seeth not as man
seeth; for man looketh on the outward appearance,
but the Lord looketh on the heart.

1 Samuel 16:7

You could go broke fixing up the outside and still be lonely and alone. Understand that what brought Samson to Delilah so often that he couldn't get up, was she became a place where he could rest.

If satan can work Delilah's strengths *against* men, then God can use them *for* men. If you are married, you can enrich your marriage through inner beauty. If you're not married, understand it's not the necklaces you wear that make you attractive. It's not the twists you put in your hair. It's something that God puts in your heart that actually affects a man.

Can you see what made Adam partake of the forbidden fruit, knowing it was evil? Eve was deceived, but he knew. Do you see how powerful your influence is? The enemy wants to capitalize on what God put in you. That is why you must watch what goes through your doors.

By Him therefore let us offer the sacrifice of praise to God continually, that is, the fruit of our lips giving thanks to His name. But to do good and to communicate forget now: for with such sacrifices God is well pleased.

Hebrews 13:15-16

True worship is born when true sacrifice occurs. When we lay upon the altar some bleeding object that we thought we would keep for ourselves (but realized it was God's all the while), that's worship. You can never be really anointed until you personally experience a situation that calls you to lay aside your garments. It is from this river that the tears of worship are born.

People who see you worship will never be able to determine why you worship by looking at things you have. It is what you left behind and laid aside that seasons you into the real aroma of worship. How much does it cost to be the "real" you? What did you lay aside to follow Him? Whatever you have laid aside, or will lay aside, determines the effectiveness of your ability to touch the world at its feet and speak to its heart!

> *For after this manner I the old time the holy women also, who trusted in God, adorned themselves... even as Sarah obeyed Abraham, calling him lord; whose daughters ye are, as long as ye do well, and are not afraid with any amazement.*
>
> 1 Peter 3:5-6

In the times of the patriarchs, they decorated themselves through their trust in God. Sarah was beautiful because she exhibited inner beauty and lived in obedience to Abraham.

You are Sarah's daughter when you are not afraid with any amazement. When you resist the temptation to react to circumstances and maintain a peaceful, meek, and quiet spirit in times of frustration, then you are Sarah's daughter.

If you can stay calm in a storm, if you can praise God under pressure, if you can worship in the midst of critics and criticism, God says you are Sarah's daughter.

If you can rebuke the fear that is knocking at the door of your heart, and tell that low self-esteem it cannot come in, you are Sarah's daughter.

If you can stand there and push a tear from off the side of your face and smile in the middle of the rain, you are Sarah's daughter.

For I say, through the grace given unto me, to every man that is among you, not to think of himself more highly than he ought to think; but to think soberly, according as God hath dealt to every man the measure of faith. For as we have many members in one body, and all members have not the same office.

Romans 12:3-4

Thank God for all the Kathryn Kuhlmans, the Oral Roberts, and the Benny Hinns whose lives have touched the world. The hot blaze of camera lights never caught the true basis of their ministry. It was the things they laid aside that made them who they were and are. Thousands are healed and saved because they did.

What about "Pastor Littlechurch" and "Evangelist Nobody" who never sold a tape or wrote a book? They paid the price nonetheless, and they are unsung heroes. Like Noah, their membership roll never exceeded eight souls, but they faithfully led them nonetheless. They wanted to do more. They thought they would go farther than they did, but they had laid aside their garments. This is the cost of Christianity stripped down to one desire, stripped to the simplicity of bareness.

Many daughters have done virtuously, but thou excellest them all.

Proverbs 31:29

God is adorning you with glory, power and majesty. He will send people into your life to appreciate your real beauty, your real essence. It is the kind of beauty that lasts in a face full of wrinkles, gray hair, falling arches, crow's feet, and all the pitfalls that may come your way. There's a beauty that you can see in a 90-year-old woman's face that causes an old man to smile. God is decorating you on the inside. He is putting a glory in you that will shine through your eyes. A man will come along and look in your eyes. He will not talk about whether they were blue or whether your eye-shadow was right or not. He will look in your eyes and see trust, peace, love, and life.

Appreciate the ornaments of God. Let God give you a new attitude. Let Him wash everything out of your spirit that is against Him. Let go of anger, hate, frustration and bitterness. God wants you unleashed. He repeats today, just as He did 2,000 years ago, *"Woman, thou art loosed."*

*For ye know the grace of our Lord Jesus Christ,
that, though He was rich, yet for your sakes He
became poor, that ye through His poverty might
be rich.*

2 Corinthians 8:9

After the last supper, Jesus did something unexpected. Jesus so loved those men that He didn't wait on them to make the first move. He laid aside His garments and He washed their feet! (See John 13:4-5.) He didn't respond to their actions—He initiated their actions. Are you always going to be a responder who only reacts to what others dictate, or are you going to initiate change in the Body? If you are going to change it, then you must be willing to be a trendsetter! You must be naked and not ashamed.

They witnessed the scene as their Master stepped down to become a servant. He laid aside His garments—not only for them, but for us all. He came to earth and stripped Himself of the glory He had with the Father before the foundations of the world!

If He were to leave a lasting impact on these men in the upper room, He must cover Himself only in a plain towel!

> Let this mind be in you, which was also in Christ
> Jesus: who, being in the form of God, thought it not
> robbery to be equal with God: but made Himself of
> no reputation, and took upon Him the form of a ser-
> vant, and was made in the likeness of men.
>
> *Philippians 2:5-7*

If you believe that God would exalt you, if you believe that you have the ability to wash the dusty sands of life from the feet of this world, then please don't join the spiritual elitists who are impressed with their own speech!

Lay aside every distraction. Lay aside your garments, wrap every naked human flaw in the warm towel of servanthood as you help others, and draw the water! But what good is that water if we fail to use it to wash away the weariness of someone's journey? God has enough water. He just needs someone who will take the risk of being the first one. He is searching for someone to lay aside his garments. Wait no longer—we are losing our generation! Lay aside your garments! The waters are drawn, my friend; we are waiting…on you!

*And let us be weary in doing well: for in due season
we shall reap, if we faint not.*

Galatians 6:9

There is nothing like a sense of time. The lack of timing is as detrimental as planting corn in the bitter winds of an Alaskan winter. There may be absolutely nothing wrong with the seed or the ground, just the time in which the farmer chose to plant.

Assuming that you understand the necessity of small beginnings, and assuming that you realize whatever you have will not replace the One who gave it and that success only creates a platform for responsibility to be enlarged—then you can begin to ascertain where you are on the calendar, the divine almanac of God. Did you know that God has an almanac? My mother always consulted the almanac to determine the best time to plant the crop she intended to harvest. It is a calendar that presents the seasons and cycles of a year. You see, the principle of seed time and harvest will not override the understanding of time and purpose. God does everything according to His eternal almanac of time and purpose!

There remaineth therefore a rest to the people of God.
Hebrews 4:9

The Sabbath is a day of rest. Rest is for the purpose of restoration. It is not just because you're tired. It is during a time of rest when you replenish or receive back those things that were expended or put out. It is during the time of restoration that the enemy wants to break off your fellowship with the Lord.

Please understand that rest and restoration are related concepts. The enemy does not want you to have rest. You need calmness or Sabbath rest because it is through the resting of your spirit that the restoration of your life begins to occur.

In the nation of Israel, God used the Sabbath day as a sign of the covenant. It proved that they were His people. They spent time in worship and fellowship with the Lord. That is the Sabbath. It is real communion between the heart of man and heart of God.

When Jesus began to minister in a restful situation, needs began to be manifested. You can never get your needs met by losing your head. When you calm down, God speaks.

For if thou altogether holdest thy peace at this time, then shall there enlargement and deliverance arise to the Jews from another place; but thou and thy father's house shall be destroyed: and who knoweth whether thou art come to the kingdom for such a time as this?

Esther 4:14

Thank God for the seasons of life He gives to His children. Mordecai taught Queen Esther an essential lesson when he spoke those words in Esther 4:14. He wanted her to realize that God had given her an opportunity to be a blessing. Now, it wasn't given to her so she could brag about the nobility of which she became a part. God isn't interested in human grandeur. When He allows us to ascend into the clouds, it is only so we can stop the rain with the enlightenment we gained from the laborious progression of our own experiences. Mordecai showed Esther that God had been grooming her all her life for this moment. In spite of the tremendous challenge set before her, she was the woman for the job. She was God's choice, a handmaiden fitly chosen and wonderfully endowed for the acquisition of a victorious report.

Create in me a clean heart, O God; and renew a right spirit within me. Cast me not away from Thy presence; and take not Thy holy spirit from me. Restore unto me the joy of Thy salvation; and uphold me with Thy free spirit.

Psalm 51:10-12

When you start murmuring and complaining, the only thing God can focus on is your unbelief. When you start resting in Him, He can focus on your problems and on the areas of your life that need to be touched.

And when Jesus saw her, He called her to Him, and said unto her, Woman, thou art loosed from thine infirmity.

Luke 13:12

Jesus healed this woman on the Sabbath. The infirm woman was not sitting around complaining. She was not murmuring. She was just sitting there listening to the words of the Master. She brought her problem with her, but her problem had not dominated her worship.

When you begin to enter into real worship with God, that's the best time to have Him minister to your needs. That's the time God does restoration in your life. Satan, therefore, wants to break up your Sabbath rest.

> *Then Esther bade them return Mordecai this answer, Go, gather together all the Jews that are present in Shushan, and fast ye for me, and neither eat nor drink three days, night or day: I also and my maidens will fast likewise; and so will I go in unto the king, which is not according to the law: and if I perish, I perish. So Mordecai went his way, and did according to all the Esther had commanded him.*
>
> *Esther 4:15-17*

Mordecai's counsel prepared Esther's mind for the purpose God had from the beginning for elevating her position. Counsel may prepare your mind, but only fervent prayer can prepare your spirit for the vast undertakings that come with it being your time. No one counsel will prepare your heart like prayer.

Esther knew that prayer undergirds the spirit and keeps a person from sagging beneath the weight of opposition. Not only did she pray, but everyone under her authority prayed as well. It is difficult to work with people who do not pray. Prayer is a strong defense against satanic attack. If Esther had not prayed, she would have fallen prey to the cunning devices of Haman, her wicked enemy!

Who being the brightness of His glory, and the express image of His person, and upholding all things by the word of His power, when He had by Himself purged our sins, sat down on the right hand of the Majesty on high.

Hebrews 1:3

Christ is our Sabbath rest. He is the end of our labors. The rest of the Lord is so complete that when Jesus was dying on the Cross, He said, *"It is finished"* (John 19:30). It was so powerful. For the first time in history, a high priest sat down in the presence of God without having to run in and out bringing blood to atone the sins of man. When Christ entered in once and for all, He offered up Himself for us that we might be delivered from sin.

If you really want to be healed, you've got to be in Him. If you really want to be set free and experience restoration, you've got to be in Him, because your healing comes in the Sabbath rest. Your healing comes in Christ Jesus. As you rest in Him, every infirmity, every area bent out of place will be restored.

No it came to pass on the third day, that Esther put on her royal apparel, and stood in the inner court of the king's house, over against the king's house: and the king sat upon his royal throng in the royal house, over against the gate of the house. And it was so, when the king saw Esther the queen standing in the court, that she obtained favor in his sight: and the king held out to Esther the golden scepter that was in his hand...

Esther 5:1-2

Esther's changing her apparel signifies our need to alter our circumstances to facilitate the success of our vision. Everything must be committed to the goal—body, soul, and spirit. When the king beheld a prepared person, he granted an expected end. He drew her into his presence because she had prepared herself for her time. There is a blessing for the person of purpose. Only the prepared will be eligible to receive this endowment from the Lord, so be ready! Ask God to give you the patience you need to become empowered to perform. Somewhere on the other side of a tremendous test is the harvest of your dream.

Rest in the Lord, and wait patently for Him: fret not thyself because of him who prospereth in his way, because of the man who bringeth wicked devices to pass.

Psalm 37:7

Sometimes it takes work to find the place of rest and calm. Our hectic world does not lend itself to quiet and peace. It creates noise and uneasiness. Even though the infirm woman of Luke 13 was bowed over and could not lift herself, she rested in the fact that she was in the presence of a mighty God. He is able to do exceedingly and abundantly above all that we may ask or think (see Eph. 3:20).

Jesus also confronted the woman at the well with some exciting truths.

Jesus therefore, being wearied with His journey, sat thus on the well: and it was about the sixth hour. There cometh a woman of Samaria to draw water: Jesus saith unto her, Give Me to drink. (For His disciples were gone away unto the city to buy meat.)

John 4:6-8

Jesus was sitting at the well waiting for someone to return. He was relaxed and calm. He knew who He was. God doesn't get excited about circumstances.

They that sow tears shall reap in joy.

Psalm 126:5

Greatness has a tremendous thirst. This thirst is quenched in the tear-stained struggle toward destiny. There will be a harvest at the end of your tears!

On the other hand, you must know when you have shed enough tears. It is important that you don't get stuck in a state of lamentation. Don't overwater the promise! Tears are for the sower, but joy is for the harvester.

Everything has a season and a purpose (see Eccles. 3:1). You need to understand that God is just and that He appropriates opportunities to advance according to His purpose. I don't know whether this is true for everyone, but usually obscurity precedes notoriety.

The first Psalm teaches that the blessed man meditates on the Word while he waits. It says that you bring forth fruit in your own season. It is good to recognize your season and prepare for it before it comes. But the fruit will not grow prior to its right season. Don't demand fruit when it is not in season. Even restaurant menus have a notation that says certain items can be served only when the fruit is in season.

I have set the Lord always before me: because He is at my right hand, I shall not be moved. Therefore my heart is glad, and my glory rejoiceth: my flesh also shall rest in hope.

Psalm 16:8-9

O ne time the disciples and Jesus were on a ship. The storm arose and appeared to be about to sink the ship. Jesus was sleeping, resting in the middle of a crisis. Everyone else was trying to figure out how they would get into life jackets. Jesus wasn't lazy. He was resting because He knew He was greater than the storm. Jesus rose up and spoke to the winds and waves and said, *"Peace, be still"* (Mark 4:39).

When you know who you are, you don't have to struggle. You don't have to wake Him up.

That was Christ's attitude when the woman at the well met Him. (See John 4.) When this woman came, she was upset about the water she needed to draw. Jesus began to demonstrate calmness and said, *"If you drink of the water that you have, you will thirst again, but if you drink of the water that I have, you will never thirst."*

And he shall be like a tree planted by the rivers of water, that bringeth forth his fruit in his season; his leaf also shall not wither; and whatsoever he doeth he doeth shall prosper.

Psalm 1:3

There may be some degree of reservation in the mind of the thinking person. "What if I enter my season and experience the rich blessings God has been promising for a long time, and then the season ends? How can I stand to go back into seclusion and be content?" All of these are excellent questions, ones that must be addressed. After all, what good is having your season if over your head gather the gloomy clouds that keep thundering a nagging threat in your ears? They threaten that all you are doing now will not last.

This is an exciting time for the prepared believer. Trained by patience and humbled by personal challenges, they will usher in a new season in the cycle of the Kingdom. Are you part of what God is doing, or are you still looking back at what God has done? I want to see you burn some spiritual rubber for Jesus!

And have put on the new man, which is renewed in knowledge after the image of Him that created him.

Colossians 3:10

When the woman at the well met Jesus, He calmly addressed her real need.

The woman answered and said, I have no husband. Jesus said unto her, Thou hast well said, I have no husband: for thou hast had five husbands; and he whom thou now hast is not thy husband: in that saidst thou truly.

John 4:17-18

Like this woman, you can get yourself into situations that wound and upset your spirit. These kinds of wounds can't be healed through human effort. You must get in the presence of God and let Him fill those voids in your life. You will not settle it up by going from friend to friend. This woman had already gone through five men. The answer is not getting another man. It's getting in touch with The Man—Jesus.

If you have something that has attached itself to you that is not of God, you won't be able to break it through your own strength. As you submit to God, you receive the power to resist the enemy.

For therein is the righteousness of God revealed from faith to faith: as it is written, The just shall live by faith.

Romans 1:17

First, let me rebuke the spirit of fear. We need to declare God to this fear. We dare not fall in love with what God is doing, but we must always be in love with who God is. God does not change. His methods may change, but His ultimate purpose doesn't. People have a need to know what comes next. God doesn't always make us privy to such information, but He has promised that if we walk uprightly, He will not withhold any good thing from us (see Ps. 84:11).

There are really no "down" times in God. We only feel down when, like spoiled children, we demand that He continue to give us what He did at one stage without appreciating the fact that we are moving from one stage to another. It is what the Word calls going from faith to faith (see Rom. 1:17).

Blessed be the God and Father of our Lord Jesus Christ, who hath blessed us with all spiritual blessings in heavenly places in Christ.

Ephesians 1:3

The woman then left...and went her way into the city, and saith to the men, Come, see a man, which told me all things that ever I did: is not this the Christ? Then they went out of the city, and came unto Him... And many more believed...and said unto the woman, Now we believe, not because of thy saying: for we have heard Him ourselves, and know that this is indeed the Christ, the Savior of the world.

John 4:28-30; 39-42

This woman ran into the city telling everyone to come and see the Man who had told her about her life. You disservice yourself until you know Jesus. He can satisfy every need and every yearning. Then He lifts every burden and every trouble in your life. God kept you living through all those years of infirmity because He had something greater for you than what you've experienced earlier. God kept you because He has something better for you. Don't give up. The blessing is on the way.

> *For this cause I have sent you Timotheus...who*
> *shall bring you into remembrance of my ways*
> *which be in Christ, as I teach every where in every*
> *church.*
>
> 1 Corinthians 4:17

Saul's greatest mistake was to fall in love with the kingdom and not the King! When God decided to move someone into his position, he tried to kill his successor. If your time as a good boxer is up, then why can't you be an excellent coach? You see, there always is an area where you can be fruitful; it simply may not be the same area all the time.

The apostle Paul began in the winter of his ministry to pour his knowledge into his successor Timothy to develop the ability to be prepared in season and out of season. I never understood this verse until another preacher began to share with me a lesson involving farming techniques.

The farmer who continuously produces crops can do so because he produces more than one type of crop. He has several different fields and he rotates a certain crop from one field to another. This coverall-clad soldier will always be productive because he understands the importance of being multifaceted.

> *...Lord, lift Thou up the light of Thy countenance upon us...I will both lay me down in peace, and sleep: for thou, Lord, only makest me dwell in safety.*
>
> *Psalm 4:6-8*

I dare you to realize that you can do all things through Christ who strengthens you (see Phil. 4:13). For example, once the infirm woman knew that she didn't have to be bent over, she stood straight up. Jesus told the woman at the well to get rid of the old: old patterns of selfishness. Suddenly, she recognized that she was healed. The sinful things that you have fought to maintain are not worth what you thought they were. Often we settle for less, but when you get the best, it gives you the power to let go of the rest.

The infirm woman that Jesus healed in Luke 13 had been in torment and pain for 18 years. When she came to Jesus, she expected that He would take care of her. The result was a wonderful healing. That's what rest and Sabbath are. They are the ability to find eternal satisfaction in Jesus. The world never gives us peace and satisfaction. Jesus offers both freely.

So God created man in His own image, in the image of God created He him; male and female created He them.

Genesis 1:27

Paul tells Timothy to be instant in season and out of season (see 2 Tim. 4:2). He then tells him to be diverse. According to his instructions, we must reprove and rebuke. We also must be able to let things rest and encourage others. I believe many people lose their sense of self-worth because they fail to diversify themselves. If we listen carefully to the voice of God, we can be productive at every stage of life. In short, diversity is a key to longevity.

Psalm 1 says that the blessed man doesn't just grow; he is also planted. Never does he "just happen." He is planted at a specific time in a specific place to accomplish a divine purpose. If you have been planted, you grow down before you grow up. God isn't concerned about how high your trunk grows. He is concerned about how deep your roots go. He has taken every struggle and test, every mishap and neglect, to cultivate in you the soil needed to make you reproductive.

Not that I have already obtained all this, or have already been made perfect, but I press on the take hold of that for which Christ Jesus took hold of me.

Philippians 3:12

Success is success only because it relates to struggle. If it were easy, anybody could do it. How can you have victory without conflict? To receive something without struggle lessens its personal value. God rewards the diligent who, through perseverance, obtain the promise. There is no way to receive what God has for your life without fighting the obstacles that block your way. In fact, people who procrastinate do so because they are desperately trying to find a way to reach the goal without going through the struggle.

When I was a kid, we used to go into the stores and change the price tags on the items we could not afford. Many people are shortchanging their spiritual life. They are attempting to get a discount on the promises of God. That doesn't work in the Kingdom. Whatever it costs, there is no swapping the price tags. You must pay your own way. You will not easily jeopardize the welfare of something not easily attained.

And the Lord said unto Cain, Why art thou wroth? and why is thy countenance fallen? If thou doest well, shalt thou not be accepted? and if thou doest not well, sin lieth at the door....

Genesis 4:6-7

People who are offended at what God does for you I call "Cain's children." Cain's children, like their father, will murder you because you have God's favor. They don't want to pay what you paid, but they want to have what you have. If you accelerate into new dimensions, however, cynicism eats at the fibers of their conversations and in their hearts.

Your enemy will not wound you because he is too far way. In order to be a good Judas, he must be at the table with the victim of his betrayal! Who sits at your table?

How many times have you prayed for a blessing and found that being blessed is hard work. Everything God gives you requires maintenance. There is a "down" side to every blessing. That is why Jesus said, *"No man builds without counting the cost"* (see Luke 14:28-30). You must ask yourself if you are willing to pay the price to get the blessing.

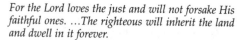

For the Lord loves the just and will not forsake His faithful ones. ...The righteous will inherit the land and dwell in it forever.

Psalm 37:28-29 NIV

There is awesome power in women. God has chosen that women serve as the vehicles through which entry is made into this world. He has shared His creativity with women. Women are strong and willing to nurture others.

In spite of this, millions of women continually suffer emotional, physical, and spiritual strain. The enemy has attempted to destroy God's vehicle of creativity. You might feel like you are alone, with no one to help you find healing.

Mistakes made early in life impact the rest of our lives. Some become involved sexually without the commitment of marriage. Perhaps you really did think that yielding would show your true love. Or, maybe, you simply wanted to have a good time without thinking about the consequences.

It could be that your emotional strain comes from having been abused. Others have taken advantage of you and used you in horrible and depraved ways. You are left feeling used and unwanted. Nevertheless, God wants you, and God's people want you.

His lord said unto him, Well done, good and faith-
ful servant; thou hast been faithful over a few
things, I will make thee ruler over many things:
enter thou into the joy of thy lord.

Matthew 25:23

Y ou must ask yourself if you are willing to pay the price to get the blessing. Another question people seldom ask themselves is whether they are willing to endure the criticism and the ridicule that come with success. Most people love the image of success, but they haven't contemplated the reality of possessing the blessing. God doesn't give us everything we ask for. The truth is, we are not ready for those things and it would probably kill us to receive what we are not prepared to maintain.

God starts His children out with what they have to teach them consistency on the level they are on. There must be an inner growth in your ability to withstand the struggles that accompany the things you have. I found out that if you really want to pursue your dream, there is a place in God whereby you build up immunity to the adversity of success. It is simply a matter of survival.

All things are yours…the world or life or death or the present or the future—all are yours, and you are of Christ, and Christ is of God.

1 Corinthians 3:21b-23 NIV

God has determined your need. He looked down from Heaven and saw your pain and guilt. He evaluated the situation and decided that you needed a Redeemer. He looked past our tendency to sin, and saw our need.

He met that need through Jesus Christ who took your abuse on Himself on the Cross of Calvary. He paid for your shame. He made a way for you to be clean again. He took all your sinful desires and crucified them on the Cross.

The abused little girl with all her wounds was healed by the stripes of Jesus (see Isa. 53:5). The sins of the woman who wanted to fulfill her lusts were crucified on the Cross with Him (see Gal. 2:20). The past is paid for. The wounds may leave scars, but the scars remind us that we are human. Everyone has scars. The circumstances of life shaped your way of thinking. God recognizes the possibility of what you can become. He has a plan.

For in the time of trouble He shall hide me in His pavilion: in the secret of His tabernacle shall He hide me; He shall set me upon a rock.

Psalm 27:5

You may be wasting precious time asking God to change the minds of people. It is not the people or the pressure that must change, it is you. In order to survive the stresses of success, you must build up immunity to those things that won't change. My constant prayer is, "Lord, change me until this doesn't hurt anymore." I am like David—I am forever praying my way into the secret place. There you are insulated from the enemy. If you want to accomplish much, if you intend to survive hate from others, then you need to get in your secret place and stay there!

What a place of solace God has for the weary heart that is bombarded with the criticism of cynical people and the pressures to perform. Many people lose their own identities in the excitement of the moment. When the excitement ebbs, as it always does, they have lost sight of the more important issues of self, home, and family!

...but the people that do know their God shall be strong, and do exploits.

Daniel 11:32b

God knows that there is a Sarah, a Rahab, a Ruth, or even a Mary in you. Hidden inside of you is a great woman who can do great exploits in His name. He wants to unleash your potential. He will spiritually stir your heart and let you know that He is moving in your life, if you will only respond to His call.

The power to unleash you is in your faith. Shift your confidence from your own weaknesses to His power. Trust in Him rather than in yourself. Anyone who comes to Christ will find deliverance and healing. He will raise you up.

He paid the price for your sin and guilt. Believe that He has washed you and made you clean. He will reward you when you call on Him and it shall be done. When you allow Him access to every area of your life, you will never be the same broken person again.

Therefore, if anyone is in Christ [s]he is a new creation; the old has gone, the new has come!

2 Corinthians 5:17 NIV

For where you have envy and selfish ambition, there you will find disorder and every evil practice.

James 3:16 NIV

Another issue is your change in values as you progress. Hopefully your morality does not change, but your sense of what is and is not acceptable should. For example, consider how differently you feel now as opposed to how you felt when you were younger. Luxuries become necessities once you become accustomed to them. Once you are exposed to certain things, it is difficult to go back to what other people might consider normal.

When the microwave was first introduced, consumers were afraid of it. Now you can't imagine not having one. Once you become accustomed to any lifestyle, it is hard to go back to what you once thought was sufficient. To add to this issue, when you move into a different place in your life, you are still surrounded by people in a former stage. Many people suffer inside because they are surrounded by others who live where they were and not where they are. These are the same types of people who called Christ the carpenter's son (see Matt. 13:55).

Yet the Lord will command His loving kindness in the daytime, and in the night His song shall be with me, and my prayer unto the God of my life.

Psalm 42:8

Who can remember when thought becomes prayer? Sometimes it changes in the middle of a sentence. Sleepless people will stare blankly out of their windows into the darkness of night. They speak the fleeting thoughts whose pattern defies grammar. Oratorical nightmares, they are just the feeble cries of a heart whose conflict has pushed the head to bow in humble submission to One greater than itself.

Understand that real prayer was not made for human ears. When we earnestly pray, we have inner feelings we didn't even know we had come to the surface. In that regard, prayer is a nausea of the mind. It brings up the unresolved past that swirls around and inside us.

Who of us would want others to hear us as we release our inner groaning before the throne? Often what we convey around others is more like a plastic-covered superficial replica of what real prayer is all about. It is a dressed-up, Sunday-go-to-meeting counterfeit that is impressive, but completely inconsequential!

For jealousy is the rage of a man: therefore he will not spare in the day of vengeance. He will not regard any ransom; neither will he ret content, though thou givest many gifts.

Proverbs 6:24-25

A s much as you need to be affirmed and understood, at some point you must ask yourself, "How much am I willing to lose in order to be accepted?" People do not always want to see you move upward. Can you endure the pressure they will put on you to come down? Be like Nehemiah, who said, *"I am doing a great work, so that I cannot come down"* (Neh. 6:3b). God may be grooming you right now for a new level by exposing you to opposition and criticism. God builds your immunity so when the greater blessing comes, you won't break.

Successful people tend to be passionate people. You can be passionate and not be successful. Passion, basically, is raw power. If it is not focused, it becomes an animalistic force. But if you can focus passion for a divine purpose, you will be successful. The central point is: "How bad do you want to be blessed?"

Whoso is wise, and will observe these things, even they shall understand the loving kindness of the Lord.

Psalm 107:43

The grandstands of Heaven behold the attempts of the righteous at piety and honor. How impressive are our sanctuaries. How stately are the auditoriums and how distinguished are the people who rush in to fill them for a punctual hour of spiritual rhetoric!

There is nothing quite comparable to the pomp and circumstance of a well-orchestrated service. Never before has there been such an emphasis placed on facilities. As glamorous as the old Catholic churches were in earlier years, they can't even compare to these space age monuments. We have manned them with people displaying the finest of administrative, musical, and oratorical abilities. Our cabinets are filled with resumés, statistics, and ledgers. We have arrived!

However, can you hear the hollow moans of the sheep who bleed behind the stained glass and upon the padded pew? I do not blame our success as the cause for their pain; neither do I suggest that the absence of ornateness would cure the ills of our society. We have majored on the minor and consequently minored on the major!

Hope deferred maketh the heart sick: but when the desire cometh, it is a tree of life.

Proverbs 13:12

How strong is your desire for accomplishment in your life? It takes more than a mere whimsical musing over a speculative end. Any man will tell you that where there is no desire, there is no passion. Where there is no passion, there is no potency. Without desire, you are basically impotent!

Desire gives you the drive you need to produce. If there is a tenacious burning desire in the pit of your stomach, you become very difficult to discourage. I have warmed my cold feet by the fires of my innermost desire to complete a goal for my life. No one knows how hot the embers glow beneath the ashes of adversity.

On a chilly morning you don't need to rebuild the fire, for beneath the ashes lie crimson embers waiting to be stirred. The fire isn't dead, but its burning isn't as brilliant as it once was. I am glad that if you have an inner desire to survive or succeed, then you only need a stirring for the embers of passion to ignite in your life.

Hear my prayer, O Lord, and give ear unto my cry;
hold not Thy peace at my tears: for I am a stranger
with Thee, and a sojourner, as all my fathers were.

Psalm 39:12

Now understand, nothing fuels prayer like need. The presence of need will produce the power of prayer. Even the agnostic will make a feeble attempt at prayer in the crisis of a moment.

Prayer is man admitting to himself that, despite of his designs and accomplishments, he needs a higher power. Prayer is the humbling of the most arrogant mind confessing, "There are still some things I cannot resolve."

Prayer is the birthplace of praise. Prayer is man acknowledging the sovereign authority of a God "who can!" You ask, "Can what?" God can do whatever He wants to do, whenever He wants to do it.

If prayer is to be meaningful, it cannot be fictitious. It must be born out of the panting of a heart that can admit its need. We must be honest enough to come before God with an open heart and a willing mind to receive what He has promised to those who are in His Word!

And the angel said unto her, Fear not, Mary: for thou hast found favor with God. And, behold, thou shalt conceive in thy womb, and bring forth a son, and shalt call His name JESUS.

Luke 1:30-31

Mary couldn't name the baby she had Jesus because she didn't fully understand His destiny. God named Jesus. Don't allow people who don't understand your destiny to name you. People also probably whispered that Jesus was the illegitimate child of Joseph. Rumors smear the reputation and defame many innocents. However, none lived with any better moral character than Jesus—and they still assaulted His reputation. Just be sure the rumors are false or in the past and keep on living. I often say, "You can't help where you've been, but you can help where you're going."

In the chilly river of Jordan, with mud between His toes, it was the voice of the Father that declared the identity of Christ. His ministry could not begin until the Father laid hands upon Him by endorsing Him in the midst of the crowd. If Jesus needed His Father's blessing, how much more do you and I? We should not seek to endorse ourselves.

*And He was there in the wilderness for forty days,
tempted of Satan; and was with the wild beasts; and
the angels ministered unto Him.*

Mark 1:13

Jesus needed ministry after being savagely attacked by
the enemy at a very vulnerable moment. After 40 days
of fasting, He was hungry (see Matt. 4:2; Luke 4:2).
Satan makes his attack when you are hungry. Hunger is a
legitimate need that satan offers to satisfy in a perverted
way. The extreme test of faith is to stand fast when you
have a *legitimate* need you could satisfy in an *illegitimate* way.

Christ seemed to have no problem rebuking the enemy
who came against Him. Some have been through so
much that they simply don't trust anymore. They need
someone, but they don't trust anyone.

Whenever we seek His will, we must be prepared to
receive His way! It is not the will of God that causes us
to struggle as much as it is the way in which He accomplishes His will. However, if the winds and rains plummet down with enough thunderous force, then we are
stripped by the struggle and brought to a place of open,
naked prayer.

...I would thou went cold or hot. So then because thou art lukewarm, and neither cold nor hot, I will spue thee out of My mouth.

Revelation 3:15-16

If the cold winds of opposition have banked the fire and your dream is dying down, I challenge you to rekindle your desire to God. Don't lose your fire. Fire manifests itself in two ways. First, it gives light. Second, fire gives heat. Fire needs fuel. Feed the fire. Feed it with the words of vision and purpose. When stress comes, fan the flames. Gather the wood. Pour gasoline if you have to, but don't let it die!

Look at the situation of Hannah, Elkanah's wife. She wanted to have a child. In order to stir up Hannah, God used a girl named Peninnah who was married to the same man but able to bear children. The more Hannah saw Peninnah have children, the more she desired her own. Peninnah provoked Hannah; she stirred Hannah's embers. It wasn't that Hannah got jealous and didn't want to see Peninnah be blessed. Other people's blessings ought to challenge you to see that it can be done.

We are hard pressed on every side, but not crushed;
perplexed, but not in despair; persecuted, but not
abandoned; struck down, but not destroyed

2 Corinthians 4:8-9 NIV

We need to get to the point where we lose our self-consciousness because we are sick and tired of allowing the enemy to subdue what God has given to us. Stripped down somewhere below our image and our name there is a power that boggles the mind. It may just be that you can't get what you need from the Lord because you are too cognizant of people and too oblivious to the presence of God.

Besides all this, we learn faith when our options diminish—who needs faith for the parting of the sea when there are bridges standing strong and erect? Faith is reserved for those times when there are no options, when "push" has collided with "shove"! There is nothing we can do but be crushed by the inevitable—or look unto the Invisible to do the impossible! Your crisis is a privilege because God has given you an opportunity to experience a deeper realm of miracle-working power!

*...For unto whomsoever much is given, of him shall
be much required: and to whom men have committed much, of him they will ask the more .*

Luke 12:48

Success cannot be defined in generalities; it can be
defined only according to individual purpose and
divine direction. Your assignment is to dig for your own
gold. Cultivate what the Lord has given to you. Find out
what you have to work with, and then work it!

There isn't a way to define success without examining
purpose. What did the inventor think when he made the
machine? Did it accomplish the purpose it was created to
perform? It doesn't matter what else it did; if it didn't
satisfy the mandate of its creator, it is unsuccessful.
When people, rather than the Creator, define success it
becomes idolatry.

The greater the blessing, the more the responsibility. It is
expensive to be blessed. Not everyone can handle the
success. Some people will never be satisfied with sitting
on the bench cheering for others who paid the price to
play the game. Inflationary times may escalate the price
of their dreams, but whatever the price, they are com-
pelled, drawn, and almost driven toward a hope.

*...and let them pray over him, anointing him with
oil in the name of the Lord: ...and the prayer of faith
shall save the sick, and the Lord shall raise him up;
and if he have committed sings, they shall be forgiven him. Confess your faults one to another, and
pray one for another, that ye may be healed....*

James 5:13-16

There is something good in you, and God knows how
to get it out. Slip the spirit of heaviness off your
shoulders. But don't put on the garment of praise just
yet. Now that you are stripped to nothing but prayer, let
your request be made known unto God.

Spread before Him every issue. He can't cleanse what
you will not expose. Bathe your mind in the streams of
His mercy.

This kind of renewal can only occur in the heart of someone who has been through enough to open his heart to
stand in the rain of His grace. Tell them that the only way
you can dress up for God is to lie before Him as a naked
offering, a living sacrifice offered up at the altar in naked
prayer!

Know ye not that they which run a race run all, but
one receiveth the prize? So run, that ye may obtain.
1 Corinthians 9:24

Distance runners take their laps and stretch their limitations, giving themselves over to committing their strength to a goal. As they near the finish line, there is a final burst of energy and they go for broke! At least once before you die, you owe it to your God and to yourself to experience in some area in your life that last-lap feeling of giving your all.

I would like to underscore a truth: huge stress comes with success in any area. For many of us there is no option. In spite of adversity, there is a pounding heart that exists in the chest of someone that says, "I will go!"

The question is universal but the answer is totally individual. Can you stand to be blessed? If yes, then the only way to be blessed is to stand! When you can't seem to put one foot in front of the other, stand. Bite your lip, taste your tears, but stand on what God showed you in the night until it happens in the light.

Additional copies of this book and other
book titles from DESTINY IMAGE are
available at your local bookstore.

Call toll-free: 1-800-722-6774.

Send a request for a catalog to:

Destiny Image₀ Publishers, Inc.
P.O. Box 310
Shippensburg, PA 17257-0310

*"Speaking to the Purposes of God for this
Generation and for the Generations to Come."*

**For a complete list of our titles,
visit us at www.destinyimage.com**